James D. Bleeker

German Navy Warships

1939-1945

W. D. G. Blundell

ALMARK PUBLISHING CO. LTD., LONDON

© 1972 Almark Publishing Co. Ltd.
Text and art work © W. D. G. Blundell

All rights reserved. No part of this publication may be reproduced, stored in a retrieval system, or transmitted by any means, electronic, mechanical, or by photo copying without prior permission from the publishers.

First Published — February 1972

ISBN 0 85524 054 7 (hard cover edition)
ISBN 0 85524 055 5 (paper covered edition)

By the same author in this series:
SHIPS OF THE ROYAL NAVY
ROYAL NAVY WARSHIPS, 1939-1945

Printed in Great Britain by
Martins Press Ltd., London EC1R 0EN
for the publishers, Almark Publishing Co. Ltd.,
270 Burlington Road, New Malden, Surrey, KT3 4NL.

Introduction

THIS book provides a comprehensive coverage of warships that served in the German Navy in World War 2. Each ship or class is represented by constant scale drawings which are reproduced to the popular international scale of 1:1200 (100 ft to the inch). Examples of all the most important ships and classes are shown in photographs. These, combined with the drawings, will give a good visual impression to all who are interested in warships. It is hoped that this book will appeal equally to warship enthusiasts, naval wargamers and warship modellers. Using these plans it would be possible to build up a complete miniature fleet in 1:1,200 scale using balsa or hardwood in the layer by layer method.

The drawings and photographs are accompanied by brief notes pointing out salient features of design and history plus basic data in standardised form giving (in order) displacement, overall length (OA) and beam, armament and speed. A short history of pre-war limiting factors and plans plus wartime developments and operations is also included.

Grateful acknowledgement is given to the Ministry of Defence (Navy), the Imperial War Museum, and A. J. North for information and photographs. Some drawings of smaller ships are larger than 1:1200 scale and in these cases an adjacent scale is provided.

CONTENTS

Section	Page
Prelude to World War Two	5
World War Two	7
Battleships	12
Battlecruisers	14
Pocket Battleships	18
Cruisers	22
Ex-World War 1 Battleships	34
Destroyers and Torpedo Boats	36
Destroyers	38
Torpedo Boats	40
Submarines	45
Aircraft Carriers and Tenders	56
Minesweepers	62
Escort Vessels	64
Landing Craft	68
Depot Ships and Supply Ships	69
Captured Ships	75
Auxiliary Cruisers	80
Minor Vessels	81
Appendices	86, 87

There was a rapid—though insufficient—build-up of the German surface fleet in the late 1930s when the various naval treaties were abrogated. Here is the launching of the cruiser Blücher with all due ceremony in 1937. The armour belt on the ship's side can be clearly seen (IWM).

FRONT COVER, TOP: A fine view of the pocket battleship Deutschland in May 1939, as freshly repainted she sailed for the coast of Spain to take part in the so-called Non-intervention Neutrality patrol. FRONT COVER, BOTTOM: Two camouflaged early 'T' series torpedo boats at speed in the Baltic in 1943.

Prelude to World War Two

WHEN World War 1 ended, Germany had a large fleet of modern, well-designed ships, though the main battle fleet had been little tested in action except for the indecisive Battle of Jutland in 1916. World War 1 had largely been a sea conflict involving submarines and commerce raiders as far as Germany was concerned—a pattern which was to be repeated on a bigger scale in World War 2. The main battle fleet, as a result, survived the war almost intact.

Under the strict terms of the Armistice, the battle fleet was dispersed, all the newest battleships, battlecruisers, cruisers and 50 destroyers being taken over by the British. A few months later, they were scuttled by their crews at Scapa Flow. Most of the other ships were taken over by France and Italy, and Germany was left with a few obsolete pre-dreadnought battleships, obsolete light cruisers, small torpedo boats and minesweepers. Thus this great ocean-going Navy was reduced to a minor coastal defence and training role.

Under the 1919 Peace Treaty terms, Germany was forbidden to have any submarines or aircraft. Any future ships were to be severely restricted in size. Maximum tonnages allowed for capital ships and cruisers were 10,000 and 6,000 tons respectively. The year 1921 saw the laying down of the first new warship with the light cruiser **Emden**, and three years later the '**Moewe**' and '**Iltis**' classes of torpedo boats were commenced. With the laying down of the **Deutschland**, in 1929, the first of the 'pocket battleships' made its appearance. On a ship of nominally 10,000 tons an armament of six 11 inch guns was to be mounted and a speed of 26 knots, faster than contemporary battleships, was called for. This was an ingenious design which kept inside the Treaty stipulations yet provided a powerful fighting ship.

Sixteen years after the end of World War 1, in 1934, the first submarines were laid down illegally, but one year later came the Anglo-German Naval Treaty. This recognized German submarines but limited their total tonnage to 45 per cent of the tonnage of submarines in the Royal Navy. Other classes of warships were limited to 35 per cent of the corresponding class in Britain which, if Germany exercised the right to build up to the limit, allowed a maximum tonnage of 184,000 tons in capital ships and 24,000 tons in submarines.

By May 1938 Hitler regarded Britain as a potential enemy and knew that the German navy would have to be considerably expanded. The 'Z' Plan called for a 'new construction' programme, ships to be ready by 1944–45:

6 battleships of 56,000 tons with 8 × 16 inch guns.
2 battleships of 42,000 tons (**Bismarck** and **Tirpitz**).
2 battlecruisers of 31,000 tons (**Scharnhorst** and **Gneisenau**).
3 battlecruisers of 31,000 tons with 6 × 15 inch guns. (Above two ships to be re-armed with 15 inch guns.)
3 pocket battleships (**Admiral Graf Spee, Admiral Scheer, Deutschland**).
2 aircraft carriers (**Graf Zeppelin** plus one projected).
126 submarines plus cruisers and destroyers.

ABOVE: Gneisenau *fires a broadside at the British aircraft carrier* Glorious *on June 8, 1940, in operations in the North Sea. Ship in foreground is* Scharnhorst. *BELOW: Commissioning ceremony for some of the first new German U-boats; Type IIA boats of the 'Weddigen Flotilla' on November 9, 1935.*

World War Two

SEVERAL units of the German navy had already put to sea and taken up their war positions, by the outbreak of war; these included the pocket battleships **Graf Spee** and **Deutschland,** naval supply ships and submarines. Their effect was soon felt with the sinking of the liner **Athenia** and the aircraft carrier **Courageous** by submarines. Scattered over the oceans were many British merchant ships, sailing alone without naval escorts and carrying no armament, and to these ships the presence of the pocket battleships constituted a serious threat.

Hastily Britain re-organised the convoy system, which had proved to be so successful in World War 1, and sent out hunting groups of warships to destroy the pocket battleships. In December 1939 the **Graf Spee,** after sinking nine merchant ships, was tracked down by the British cruisers **Ajax, Achilles** and **Exeter,** and damaged in battle; to avoid being destroyed, on Hitler's orders, she was scuttled off the River Plate. After sinking two merchant ships the **Deutschland** returned to Germany and the convoy system, now in operation, counteracted to a certain extent the submarine threat. Other naval activity in 1939 included the sinking of the British battleship **Royal Oak** at anchor at Scapa Flow by the U47, which had skilfully penetrated the harbour defences, and the destruction of the hopelessly out-gunned armed merchant cruiser **Rawalpindi** by the **Scharnhorst** and **Gneisenau.**

In April 1940 Germany invaded Denmark and Norway which brought about several actions between the British and German navies. At the first battle in Narvik fjord a superior force of German destroyers sank two British destroyers and badly damaged others for the loss of two **'Von Roeder'** class destroyers. Three days later, on April 13, the British exacted a terrible retribution when the battleship **Warspite** and destroyers which entered the fjord sank eight destroyers of the **'Von Roeder'** and **'Leberecht Maass'** classes. Two other ships of the **'Leberecht Maass'** class were sunk by mines off the Norwegian coast on April 22; in less than two weeks more than half the destroyers in the German navy at that time, 12 ships out of 22 had been lost. Other serious

An early set-back to German naval fortunes in World War 2 came with the scuttling of the pocket battleship Graf Spee *off Montevideo on December 17, 1939, after the engagement with a British cruiser force off the River Plate (IWM).*

The U-boats were beaten in the latter half of the war by Britain's development of air cover for convoys (by escort carrier or long-range aircraft) and the use of radar and well-tried tactics by convoy escort groups. In April 1945, when this picture was taken, no U-boat was safe on the surface until, like this Type VIIA, it reached the range of German shore-based aircraft. This view is from the nose of a patrolling Heinkel III.

casualties in this bitter campaign included the cruisers **Blucher, Konigsberg** and **Karlsruhe** which meant that one-third of the small cruiser force available had been lost.

During this campaign the **Scharnhorst** and **Gneisenau** inflicted considerable damage upon the British navy by sinking the aircraft carrier **Glorious,** caught on her way home after operations in Norway, and her escorting destroyers **Ardent** and **Acasta.** Another British destroyer, the gallant little **Glowworm,** went down fighting against the **Admiral Hipper.** Several other British warships were sunk off Norway by the German air force. There is little doubt that Hitler began to lose faith in his surface ships with the serious losses that had been incurred in the Norwegian campaign.

For the rest of the war the part played by surface warships was to be completely overshadowed by the ever increasing submarine activity. In many ways this was to be expected, as submarines could be produced comparatively quickly and, perhaps more important, did not require such large numbers of trained personnel to man them. However, before leaving the surface scene, the following incidents are worthy of note.

In 1940–41 the **Scharnhorst** and **Gneisenau** made raids in the Atlantic, sinking 22 merchant ships totalling over 115,000 tons, and the smaller **Admiral Scheer,** in the Atlantic and Indian Oceans, sank 17 ships totalling over 113,000 tons. During the first half of the war armed raiders took a large toll of Allied shipping. These were specially selected fast merchant ships that relied upon their mercantile appearance for disguise. Most were given quite a powerful armament, hidden completely but easily available for use, comprising $6 \times 5{\cdot}9$ inch guns, torpedo tubes and two aircraft. Ten of these ships broke out at various intervals and, between them, sank 131 merchant ships and the Australian cruiser **Sydney.** It was impossible to sustain these operations without overseas bases and supply ships which were being intercepted in

The daring Channel dash of February 1942 was a morale-booster for Germany's battered surface fleet and emphasized the low level of Britain's fortunes at that time. Here the destroyer escort is seen from Prinz Eugen *as they hug the French coast.*

ever increasing numbers by the Allies.

The **Bismarck,** with her huge potential destructive power, was the last real gamble by the German Navy to prove the case for the large surface raider. Although she sank the large battlecruiser **Hood** and went down fighting impossible odds she had completely failed in her mission which, from the outset, had been to break out into the Atlantic and destroy merchant ships. As far as Hitler was concerned this was the end of the capital ship and all future naval operations were to be concentrated on submarines.

No more surface ships were built. Gone were the grandiose building schemes envisaged before the war—some of these ships had actually been laid down, but no replacements were forthcoming for the serious losses that had been incurred. Attention was focused on the **Scharnhorst, Gneisenau** and **Prinz Eugen,** in February 1942, when these three ships boldly broke out of Brest and sailed successfully through the English Channel to Germany. A forlorn sortie by the **Scharnhorst,** in December 1943, led to her destruction by the British battleship **Duke of York.** In Norway the **Tirpitz** remained a potential threat to Russian convoys until she was finally sunk by bombing at the end of 1944.

Commerce raiding was the main activity of the German surface fleet in the early part of the war. Here the crew of a twin 4·1 inch gun watch a British merchantman go to the bottom after it had been attacked by gunfire. German ship is unidentified but is probably Scharnhorst.

With the exception of the **Prinz Eugen** and **Nurnberg** all remaining capital ships and cruisers had been reduced to wrecks by bombing.

Due to the restrictions of the World War 1 Armistice and Naval Treaties there were only 57 submarines available when the war commenced. Then it was visualised that their mode of operations would be, as in World War 1, to patrol submerged during the day and to surface at night. Contributing factors were slow underwater speed and a small underwater range which was due to

Vulnerable to British air attacks, Tirpitz *spent a long period holed up in a Norwegian fiord. Note the torpedo nets which did not prevent an attack by British midget submarines (MoD).*

battery-driven electric motors which had to be recharged. At night, when it was safer to surface, the batteries were recharged and a much higher surface speed was given by the more powerful diesel engines.

For the first part of the war, submarines generally acted as single units but later, as convoys grew in size, groups were formed—'Wolf Packs'—in order to inflict heavier losses by a greater concentration of torpedoes. Larger and longer range boats were built, some of which went as far as Japan. To support operational boats at sea special types were developed for carrying extra fuel and torpedoes; to partially overcome the strict Allied blockade some pure cargo carriers were made. Throughout the war the standard and most numerous boat was the type VII, which with various modifications and improvements was made throughout the war.

By 1943 the Allies had air cover at sea, more experience in anti-submarine warfare, better escort ships and radar in common use. Heavy losses were being inflicted on the submarines which were being forced to stay submerged for much longer periods. To counteract these disadvantages the schnorkel was introduced. This was a ventilation device, originally being developed in Holland in 1940 but taken over by the Germans, which enabled the diesel engines to be used whilst submerged at shallow depths. Marginal improvements were made on underwater speed by removing guns from many boats. Mass production of boats by prefabrication methods was introduced to compensate for the heavy losses at sea.

Eventually, in the desperate search for high underwater speed, the Walter turbine was developed. This was a closed circuit gas driven turbine; hydrogen peroxide mixed with water produced a hot gas to drive the turbine, which gave high speed at the cost of high fuel consumption. Experimental boats, with streamlined hulls, were fitted with this unit and trials carried out; types XVII and XVIII were developed to take this unit but the war ended before they became operational. During the course of the war more than 1,000 submarines were made and of these over 600 were sunk.

From a naval viewpoint Germany went to war before she had enough warships built to oppose Britain, a great maritime power. The inadequate number of large warships was never added to, as had been sensibly planned before the war, nor were the totally unexpected losses ever replaced. Consequently the surface arm virtually ceased to function quite early in the war and all efforts were concentrated on submarines. Great strides were made in this sphere but, due to the overwhelming superiority, losses soon exceeded building which was increasingly hampered by bombing. Nothing could replace the loss of experienced sailors who, despite the material limitations and lack of political forethought, did their best with what was available and fought doggedly to the end.

Battleships

Bismarck (in action against Hood) 5/1941

BISMARCK (1939), TIRPITZ (1939)

Displacement:	42,000 tons approximately.
Dimensions:	792 (OA) × 118.
Armament:	8 × 15 inch, 12 × 5·9 inch, 16 × 4·1 inch, 16 × 37mm. 8 torpedo tubes. 4 aircraft.
Speed:	30 knots, 138,000 SHP.
Complement:	2,400.

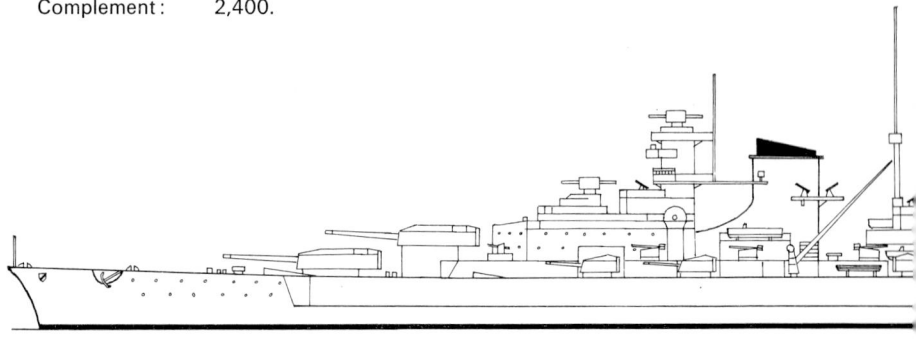

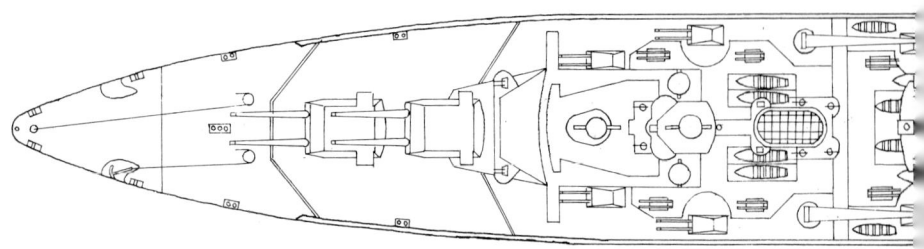

Bismarck (above)　　　　　　　　　　　　　　　Tirpitz (below)

These were the largest ships ever built for the German navy and, in order to comply with treaty regulations, their tonnage was originally announced as 35,000 tons.

On May 21, 1941 the **Bismarck** sailed from Bergen with the **Prinz Eugen** to intercept convoys in the Atlantic. A massive operation was launched by the British to track down and destroy this ship. Three days later the **Hood** was sunk and the **Prince of Wales** damaged by the **Bismarck's** guns. However, this initial success was short lived and on May 27 the **Bismarck** went down fighting against the **King George V** and **Rodney,** having suffered earlier damage by Swordfish aircraft from the **Victorious** and **Ark Royal.**

The career of the **Tirpitz** was not as spectacular but her presence in Norwegian waters caused the scattering of the British convoy PQ17 and the subsequent loss of most of the merchant ships in it. Such a threat to the Russian convoys had to be removed but, in the event, this proved to be harder than the British expected. On September 23, 1943 damage was inflicted by midget submarines; in 1944 she was further damaged by three air strikes from aircraft carriers, and towards the end of the year further damage was caused by RAF bombers and finally, on November 12, 1944 she was again bombed by the RAF and capsized off Tromso.

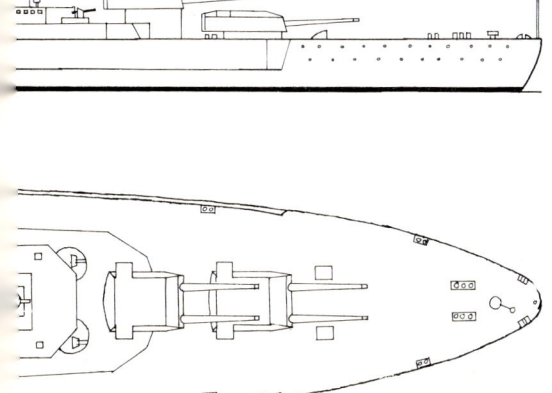

Bismarck *had higher, more prominent foremast and small mast aft ahead of after director. Drawing shows original design. Prominent searchlight platforms subsequently mounted each side of funnel in bulbous sponsons — see pictures.*

Battlecruisers

SCHARNHORST (1936), GNEISENAU (1936)

Displacement: 32,000 tons.
Dimensions: 742 (OA) × 98.
Armament: 9 × 11 inch, 12 × 5·9 inch, 14 × 4·1 inch, 16 × 37mm, plus 20mm, 6 torpedo tubes, 4 aircraft.
Speed: 31·5 knots, 160,000 SHP.
Complement: 1,800.

Designed as battlecruisers, these large ships suffered from an inadequate main armament, although plans were made to re-equip them with 6 × 15 inch guns in three turrets of two guns each.

For the first part of the war these two ships sailed together and built up an impressive record. In November 1939 they sank the armed merchant cruiser **Rawalpindi**; seven months later the aircraft carrier **Glorious** and destroyers **Ardent** and **Acasta** were sunk. Raiding in the Atlantic, in 1941, they destroyed 22 merchant ships before putting into Brest. There they were bombed regularly by the RAF until it was decided that these valuable ships had to be moved to a safer harbour. Together with the cruiser **Prinz Eugen** they made a spectacular dash up the English Channel and, as they had taken the British completely by surprise, brushed aside all opposition that was put up in the form of attacks by aircraft and small craft. This was to be their last voyage together.

A few months later, the 11 inch turrets of the **Gneisenau** were removed, two went to Norway and one to Holland, and a refit was begun which would include the long-delayed fitting of 15 inch guns. However, due to material and labour shortages, the refit was abandoned and the hulk was sunk as a blockship at Gdynia in March 1945; the hulk was finally broken up by the Russians after the war.

After the Channel dash, during which she suffered damage from mines, the **Scharnhorst** was repaired and sent to Norway. There she was a threat to Russian convoys until December 1943 when she was intercepted by a British force which included the battleship **Duke of York**. The 11 inch guns were no match for the British 14 inch guns which were directed by radar and the **Scharnhorst** went down gallantly fighting to the end.

Gneisenau (original straight stem) IWM-HU1036 1937

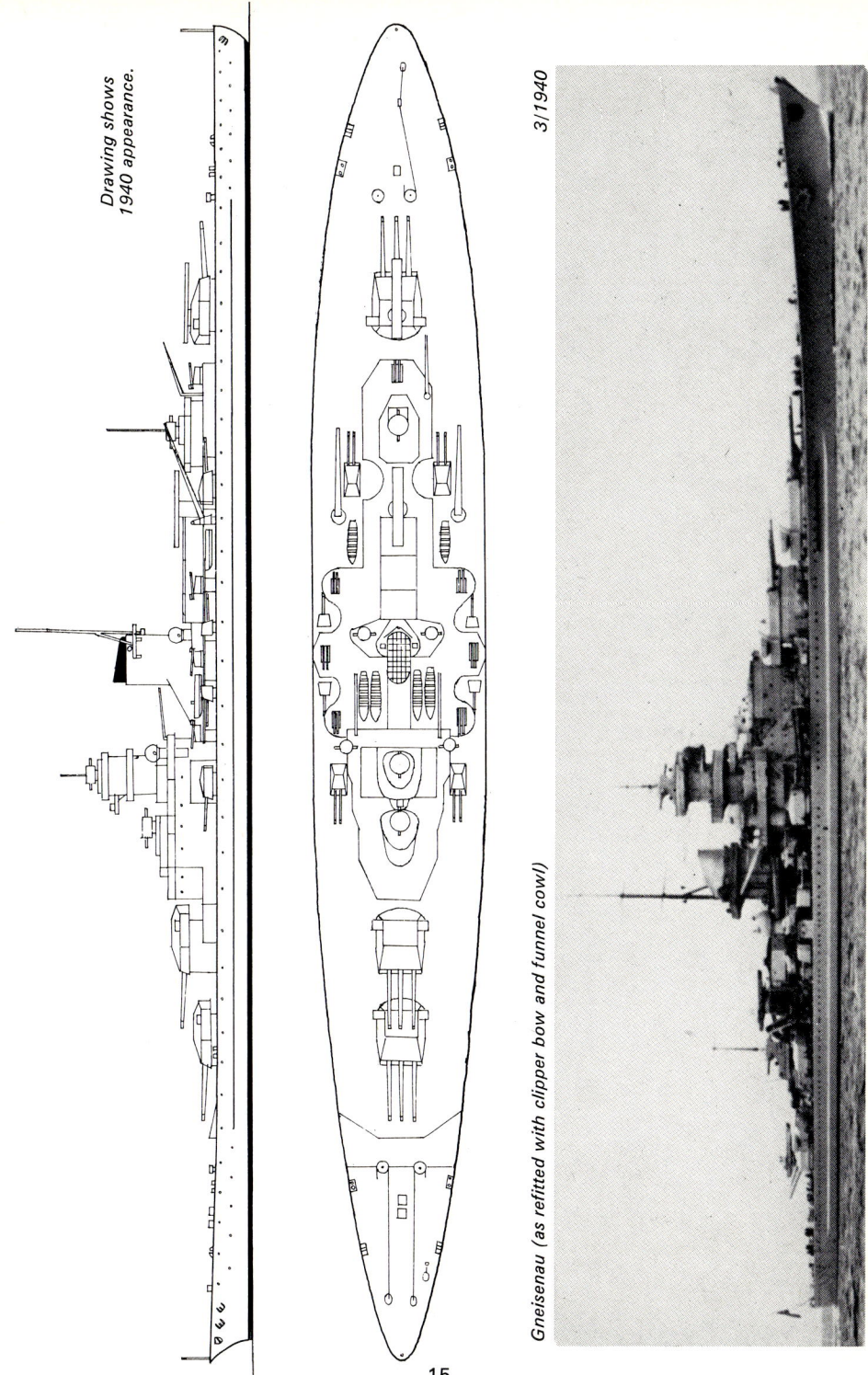

Drawing shows 1940 appearance.

Gneisenau (as refitted with clipper bow and funnel cowl) 3/1940

Scharnhorst (as built with straight stem)   1937

Gneisenau   1937

Gneisenau   1941

Morning colours and divisions aboard the Scharnhorst *in 1938 showing the 11 inch turret with superimposed aircraft catapult. Note also the stern decoration and stream anchor.*

Note: These ships were originally built and commissioned in 1936–37 with straight cruiser stems. Just prior to World War 2 they were modified with clipper bows and slightly increased forward sheer to improve sea-keeping qualities. A funnel cowl was added to keep smoke from the gunnery direction equipment. Later the forward aircraft catapult was removed.

Pocket Battleships

Deutschland 1939

DEUTSCHLAND (1931), ADMIRAL SCHEER (1933), ADMIRAL GRAF SPEE (1934)

Displacement: 12,100 tons. **Deutschland** 11,700 tons.
Dimensions: 609 (OA) × 70. (**Deutschland** beam $67\frac{1}{2}$).
Armament: 6 × 11 inch, 8 × 5·9 inch, 6 × 4·1 inch, 8 × 37mm. (**Scheer** and **Lutzow** had many 20mm guns added.) 8 torpedo tubes, 2 aircraft.
Speed: 26 knots, 56,000 BHP (Diesels).
Complement: 1,150.

The announcement of these three ships caused considerable interest and amazement when it was learnt that Germany was building capital ships on only a 10,000 tons displacement. Their main features were:
 (a) A heavy armament of 11 inch guns.
 (b) A higher speed than contemporary battleships.
 (c) A large radius of action achieved by diesel engines.
These features combined meant that they could out-gun all cruisers and out-run all battleships and make ideal merchant ship raiders. However, it was

Admiral Graf Spee (note false bow wave) MoD 12/1939

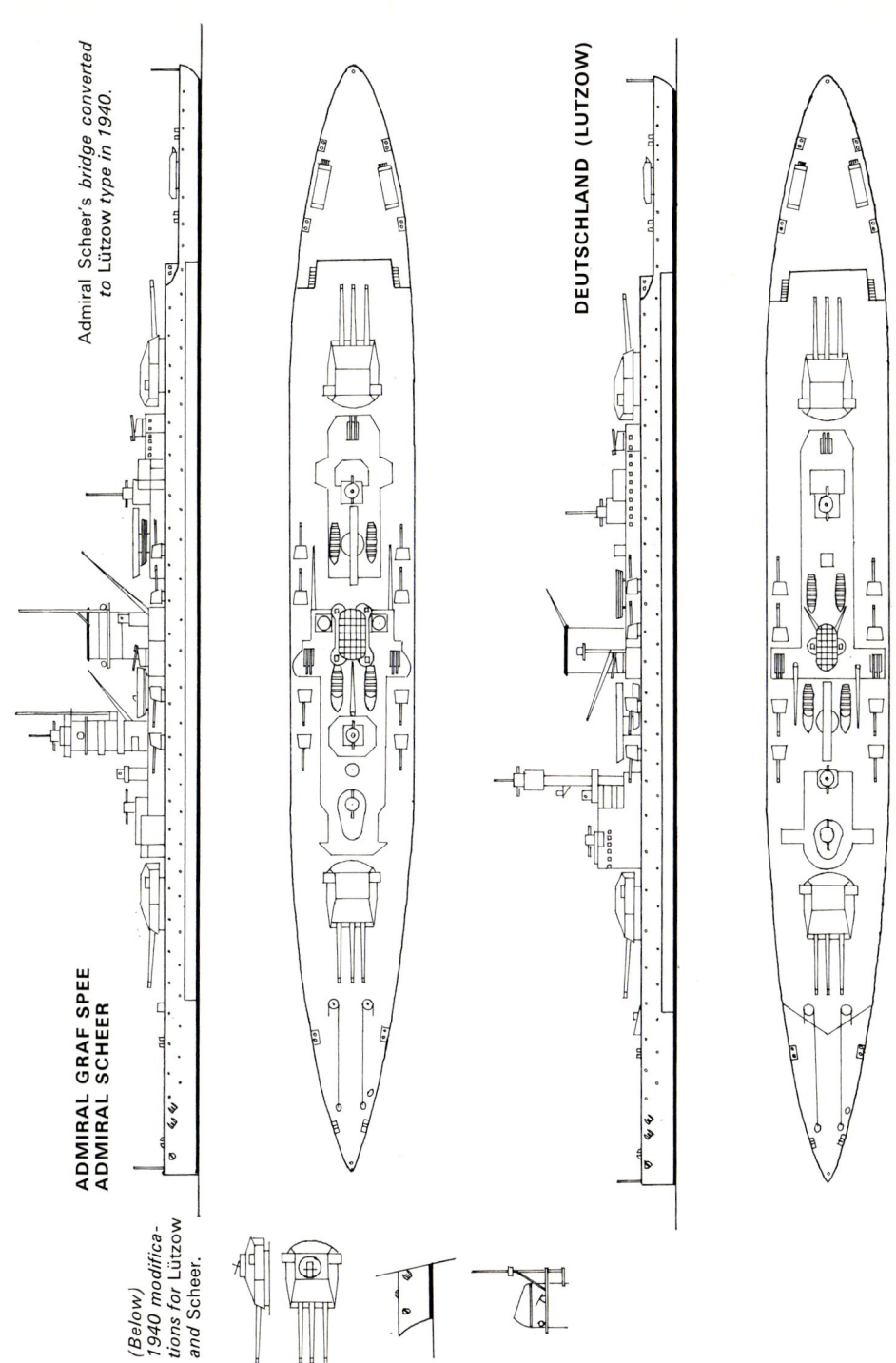

Deutschland IWM-HU1033 1932

ceded that the three British and two French battlecruisers were the only ships that could possibly destroy them.

Ten days before the war commenced the **Deutschland** and **Admiral Graf Spee** put to sea with the object of raiding in the Atlantic if Britain declared war. Two months later the **Deutschland** returned to Germany after sinking only two ships, although her presence had created a serious threat. For a while her sister ship had greater luck, sinking nine ships in the Atlantic and Indian Oceans and, at the same time, committing many ships of the Royal Navy to search thousands of miles for her. On December 13, 1939, she was caught by the cruisers **Ajax, Achilles** and **Exeter** and damaged in the ensuing battle. After putting into Montevideo, for hasty repairs, a political decision was made to scuttle her rather than risk losing a battle at this early stage of the war.

Admiral Scheer IWM-HU1031 1939

Deutschland   4/1939

In February 1940 the **Deutschland** was renamed **Lutzow** and with the **Admiral Scheer** was reclassified as a heavy cruiser; at the same time both ships were refitted with clipper bows, funnel caps and the **Scheer** was given a lighter bridge structure. In October 1940 the **Scheer** broke out into the Atlantic and Indian Oceans for five months and during this period sank 17 ships, including the armed merchant cruiser **Jervis Bay,** totalling just over 113,000 tons. Both ships saw active service in Norwegian waters and, towards the end of the war, supported army operations in the Baltic. The **Lutzow** was scuttled on May 4, 1945 after bomb damage and the **Scheer** capsized after RAF bombing in Kiel on April 9, 1945.

Deutschland   1935

Cruisers

Admiral Hipper (as built)   MoD   *1939*

'Hipper' class
ADMIRAL HIPPER (1937), BLUCHER (1937), PRINZ EUGEN (1938), SEYDLITZ (1939), LUTZOW (1939)

Displacement: 13,900 tons.
Dimensions: 654 (OA) × 71.
Armament: 8 × 8 inch, 12 × 4·1 inch, 12 × 37mm, plus 20mm, 12 torpedo tubes, 3 aircraft.
Speed: 32 knots, 132,000 SHP.
Complement: 1,600.

    According to Treaty limitations these ships were supposed to be only 10,000 tons but in the event exceeded this figure considerably. The last two named ships never had an active career with the German navy: in 1940 the **Lutzow** was sold to the USSR and subsequently destroyed by German bombers at Leningrad in 1942. The **Seydlitz**, before completion as a cruiser had been carried out, was taken in hand for conversion to an aircraft carrier but this was not proceeded with and she was scuttled at the end of war at Konigsberg.
    Shore batteries and torpedoes, in Oslo Fjord, sank the **Blucher** in April 1940.
    The other two ships had much more active careers. In April 1940 the **Hipper** was rammed by the British destroyer **Glowworm** before the smaller ship was

Admiral Hipper (as built)   MoD   *1939*

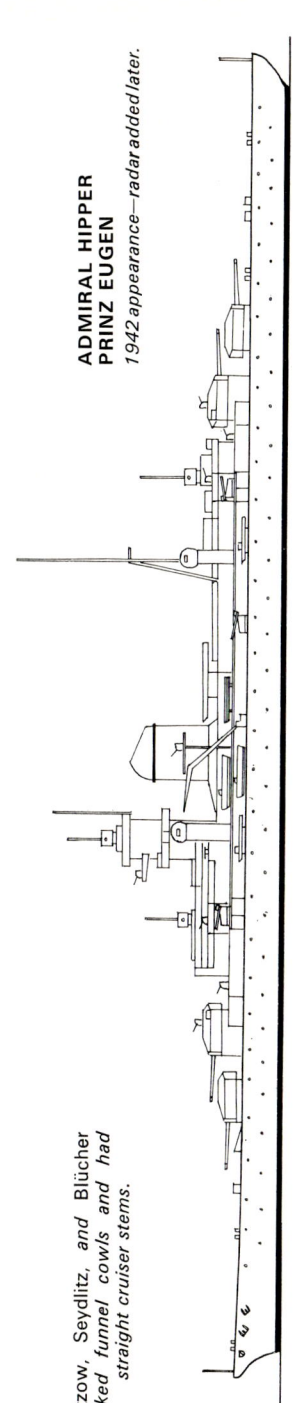

Lützow, Seydlitz, and Blücher lacked funnel cowls and had straight cruiser stems.

ADMIRAL HIPPER PRINZ EUGEN

1942 appearance—radar added later.

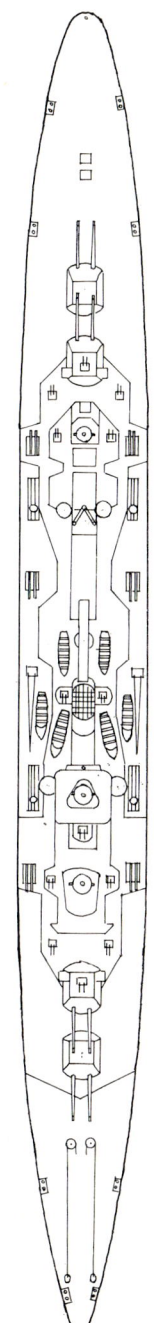

1/1946

Prinz Eugen *(with funnel cowl and clipper bow)*

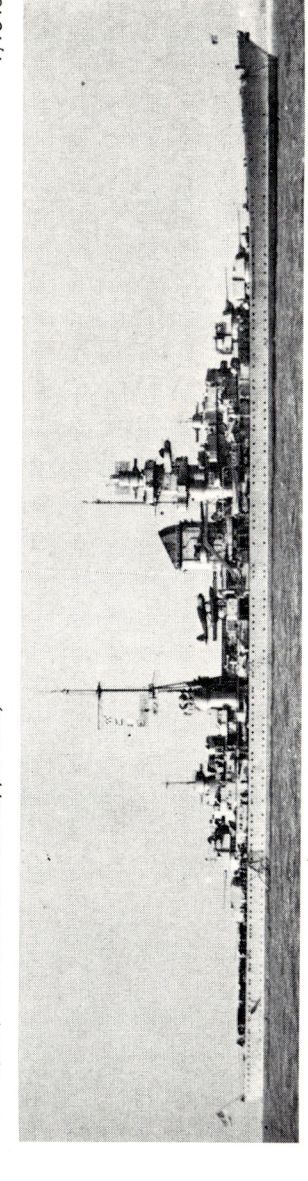

Like other major German surface vessels, the survivors of this class were refitted in 1941-42 with clipper bows and funnel cowls.

Prinz Eugen   MoD   *1/1946*

sunk. Later in the year she went out into the North Atlantic and sank 12 merchant ships totalling over 66,000 tons. For the next two years she remained in Norway as a threat to Russian convoys and, aftet these duties, supported land operations in the Baltic before being scuttled in Kiel at the end of the war. After the **Bismarck** had been sunk the **Prinz Eugen** went to Brest and from there took part in the famous English Channel dash with the two battlecruisers. She gave support in the Baltic to land operations and was surrendered intact; in 1947 she was destroyed by Atomic bomb trials at Bikini.

NURNBERG

Displacement:	6,980 tons.
Dimensions:	603 (OA) × 54.
Armament:	9 × 5·9 inch, 8 × 3·5 inch, 8 × 37mm, 12 torpedo tubes 2 aircraft.
Speed:	32 knots, 66,000 SHP.
Complement:	896.

Launched in 1934 this was the last of the light cruisers to be completed although, as mentioned earlier, the pre-war programmes called for more ships of this category. Her war career included service in Norway and the Baltic. At the end of the war she was allocated to the USSR and served as the **Admiral Makarov** until scrapped in 1959.

Nürnberg   *6/1937*

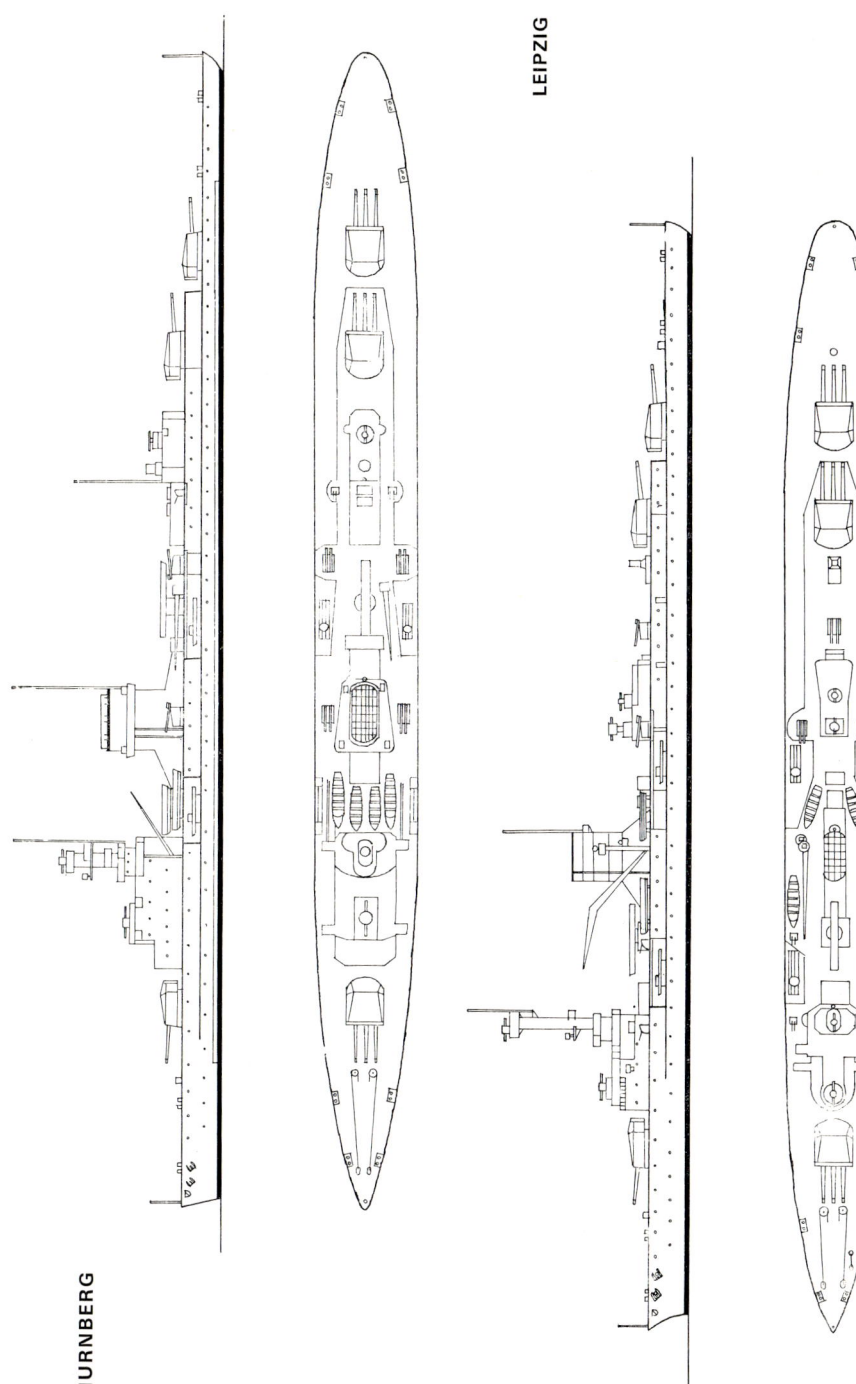

Leipzig (and aft detail of Königsberg)   1934

As built, Leipzig *had two single 37mm AA guns on 'X' gun deck; in 1937 these were replaced by a twin 3·5 inch mount as shown in drawing (page 25) and upper picture opposite.*

Leipzig   1937

Leipzig 4/1939

LEIPZIG

Displacement:	6,710 tons.
Dimensions:	580 (OA) × 53.
Armament:	9 × 5·9 inch, 8 × 3·5 inch, 8 × 37mm, 12 torpedo tubes, 2 aircraft.
Speed:	32 knots, 66,000 SHP.
Complement:	850.

Launched in 1929 this ship was similar to the '**Koln**' class but had her two funnels trunked into one, and the 5·9 inch gun turrets were mounted on the centre line. Although not sunk during the war the **Leipzig** was dogged with bad luck. In December 1939 she was torpedoed by the British submarine **Salmon** and badly damaged. Nearly four years later, whilst supporting land operations in the Baltic, she was again badly damaged when the **Prinz Eugen** collided with her. Too damaged to be of use to the Allies she was finally sunk in the North Sea, loaded with unwanted poison gas, in 1946.

Leipzig IWM-HU1022 1934

Leipzig (forward detail)   4/1939

KOLN (1928), KONIGSBERG (1927), KARLSRUHE (1927)

Displacement: 6,650 tons.
Dimensions: 570 (OA) × 50.
Armament: 9 × 5·9 inch, 6 × 3·5 inch, 8 × 37mm, 12 torpedo tubes, 2 aircraft.
Speed: 32 knots, 68,000 SHP.
Complement: 820.

An unusual feature of these ships was the staggered rear 5·9 inch gun turrets which was necessitated by the position of the rear magazines. As well as steam turbines all three ships, in common with the two later light cruisers, had diesel engines fitted for economical cruising.

The **Koln** was the only ship of this class to serve until almost the end of the war when she was bombed and sunk in Wilhemlshaven in April 1945. Prior

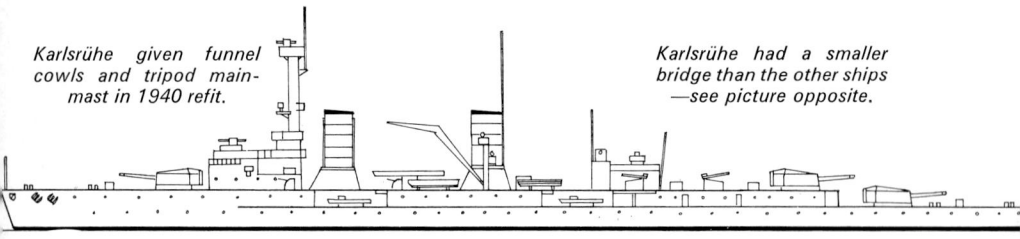

Karlsrühe given funnel cowls and tripod mainmast in 1940 refit.

Karlsrühe had a smaller bridge than the other ships —see picture opposite.

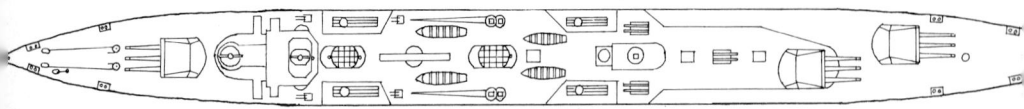

Königsberg   1934

to this she had served in Norway and also gave support to land operations in the Baltic. On April 10, 1940 the **Konigsberg** was dive bombed and sunk by Skuas of the Fleet Air Arm; in 1943 the wreck was raised but capsized later and was broken up. The **Karlsruhe** met her fate on the same day as the **Konigsberg,** being badly damaged by the British submarine **Truant** and later sunk by her own forces.

Karlsrühe   6/1939

Königsberg 8/1935
Köln 4/1939

Köln   *4/1939*

EMDEN

Displacement: 5,600 tons.
Dimensions: 508 (OA) × 47.
Armament: 8 × 5·9 inch, 3 × 3·5 inch, 4 × 37mm, 4 torpedo tubes.
Speed: 29 knots, 46,000 SHP.
Complement: 630.

    Launched in 1925, named after the famous raider of World War 1, this light cruiser was the first large warship built by Germany after the 1918 Armistice.

Emden   *1932*

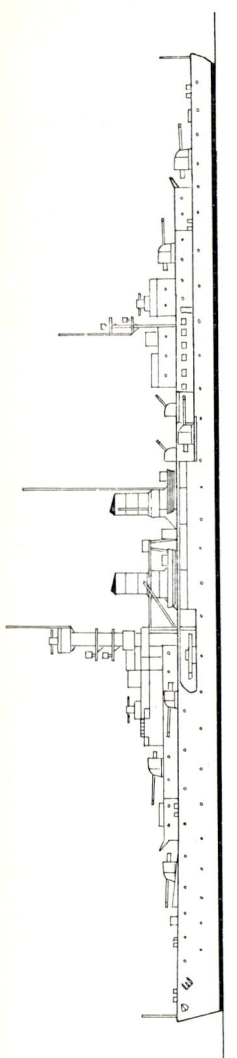
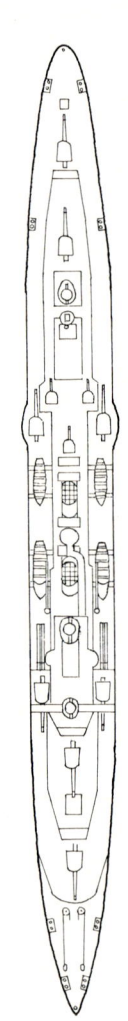

Drawing shows appearance c. 1942

Emden

IWM-HU1018

1939

Her design was considerably influenced by the later cruisers built in World War 1 and, with single gun mountings and poor AA defence, was obsolescent by the time she was completed. Before the war she performed useful service as a training ship, making several foreign cruises. Her war service included the Norwegian campaign and operations in the Baltic against the Russians; in April 1945 she was damaged by bombs in Kiel and scuttled there shortly afterwards.

Target Ship (ex-cruiser)

Hessen (Hannover in background)   9/1934

HESSEN (1904/1935)

Displacement: 13,200 tons.
Dimensions: 419 (OA) × 72.
Speed: 18 knots.

Hessen was one of several **'Braunschweig'** class cruisers of old obsolete type which Germany was allowed by the 1921 Peace Treaty. In the 1930s these were gradually scrapped except for **Hessen** which, in 1935, was converted to a radio-controlled target ship for aerial bombing training. The old battleship **Hannover** was similarly converted—see next page. **Hessen** was captured by the Russians in 1945 and transferred to their fleet for a short time. The gun turrets were removed when the vessel was converted.

Schleswig Holstein   10/1937

Old Battleships

SCHLESIEN, SCHLESWIG HOLSTEIN, HANNOVER

Displacement: 13,040 tons.
Dimensions: 413 (OA) × 73.
Armament: 4 × 11 inch, 10 × 5·9 inch, AA guns added during the war included 4·1 inch, 40 and 20mm.
Speed: 16 knots.
Complement: 725.

    Launched in 1906, these three ships saw service in World War 1, including the Battle of Jutland. By the terms of the Peace Treaty Germany was allowed to keep these old ships, which were used for cadet training duties. **Schlesien** and **Schleswig Holstein** fired the first naval shots of World War 2 at Hela and Westerplatte in Poland. The Baltic remained their sphere of operations throughout the war, where they gave support to the army against the Russians. Even after the **Schleswig Holstein** was bombed and sunk, in shallow water, at Gdynia she continued to lend her fire power to the army until she was scuttled in March 1945. A few days before the war ended the **Schlesien** was mined off Swinemunde and four years later was finally broken up. The **Hannover** was converted to a radio-controlled target ship in 1935 but was little used, and became a training and accommodation hulk. It was scrapped in 1946.

SCHLESIEN *(inset)* **SCHLESWIG HOLSTEIN**

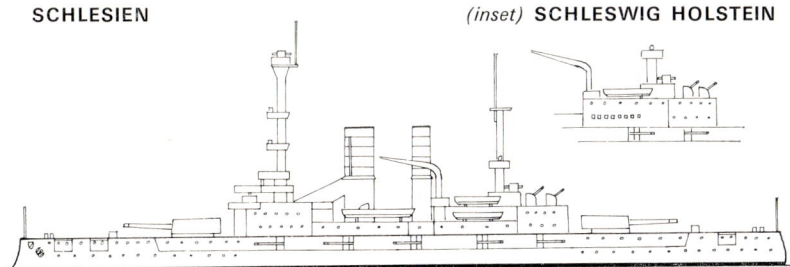

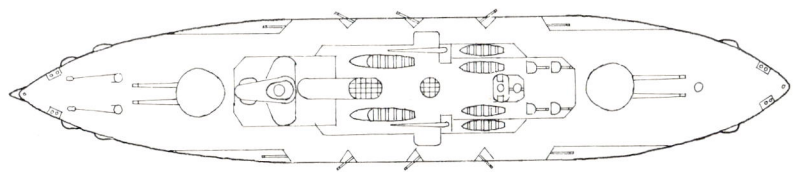

In the last year of the war as the Allied offensive closed in, the Kriegsmarine's surface and underwater fleets, already hemmed in by Allied command of the seas, was severely decimated by attacks on major harbours. This is Admiral Hipper, *bombed in dry dock at Kiel in May 1945, a sad end to a once-proud fleet of fine warships (IWM).*

Destroyers and Torpedo Boats

THERE was always a certain amount of confusion between these two types of warships so the following explanatory paragraphs have been included.

Towards the end of the nineteenth century the torpedo boat—small, fast and primarily armed with torpedoes—was introduced in most navies, and its main target was the capital ship. To counteract this menace the torpedo boat destroyer was evolved which, in practise, turned out to be a larger type torpedo boat armed with torpedoes and heavier guns than the smaller boats. Eventually the destroyer, its full name having been shortened, took over the original torpedo attack role completely, and also took on other duties which included escort work. However, the term torpedo boat lingered on in some navies, but a more accurate description, in the case of most German torpedo boats, would have been small destroyers. It is interesting to note that pre-war plans included, some of these ships were actually on the stocks but never completed, destroyers up to 480 ft with 6 × 5·9 inch guns and torpedo boats up to 358 ft with 4 × 5 inch guns.

German destroyers were, as a whole, larger and more heavily armed than their British counterparts. Some of the later ones, armed with 5·9 inch guns,

In the early days of the war before the convoy system was well organized, there were still opportunities for commerce raiding. Here a 'Leberecht Maass' class destroyer manoeuvres to pick up survivors after torpedoing a 3,000 tons gross British merchantman in the North Sea.

Z39 ('Narvik' class)　　　IWM-HU3302　　　1942

were almost light cruisers, but lacked the radius of action to carry out this role properly. More than half the pre-war force, ships of the **'Von Roeder'** and **'Leberecht Maass'** classes, was destroyed in the Norwegian campaign of 1940. Further war service included attacks on Russia-bound convoys from Norwegian bases, during which the Z16 and Z26 were lost. Some were lost in action in the English Channel and the Bay of Biscay and these included the Z8, Z27 and Z32. During the last bitter year of the war many were used in the Baltic against the Russians, where losses included the Z35 and Z36. The few survivors were allocated to Britain, France and Russia after the war. (Note: All destroyers were prefixed with the letter Z and the pre-war ships had names as well.) Most torpedo boats were prefixed with the letter T; those built before 1939, the **'Wolf'** and **'Mowe'** classes, had names and letters. Their war service was carried out in the same theatres as destroyers and the following ships were lost: all the **'Wolf'** and **'Mowe'** classes, T1, 2, 3, 5, 6, 7, 10, 13, 15, 16, 18, 22, 24, 25, 26, 27, 29, 30, 31, 32, 34 and 36.

Ships of the **'Von Roeder'** and **'Leberecht Maass'** classes sunk at the first and second battles of Narvik are indicated by an asterisk (*) in their data notes.

Z25 ('Narvik' class)　　　IWM-HU1053　　　1942

Z37 ('Narvik' class) IWM-HU3272 1944

Z24, Z26, Z28, Z30, Z31, Z33 had single gun forward.

'Narvik' class

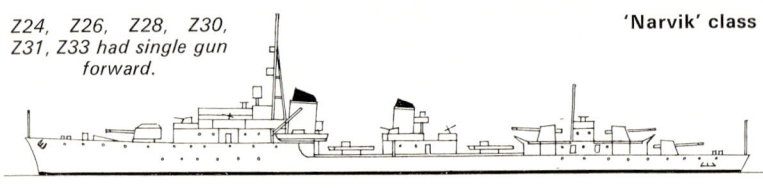

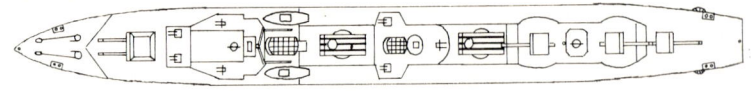

'Narvik' class (17 ships)
Z23, 25, 27, 29, 32, 34, 37, 38 and 39
Main armament: 5 × 5·9 inch guns (turret).
Z24, 26, 28, 30, 31 and 33
Main armament: 4 × 5·9 inch guns (single mounts).
Z35 and 36
Main armament: 5 × 5 inch guns (single mounts, two forward).
Displacement: 2,600 tons.
Dimensions: 390 (OA) × 40.
Armament: See above plus 4 × 37mm, various 20mm, 8 torpedo tubes.
Speed: 38 knots, 70,000 SHP.
Complement: 320. Built: 1939-42.

Friedrich Ihn IWM-HU3271 1940

Richard Beitzen   IWM-HU1051   1940

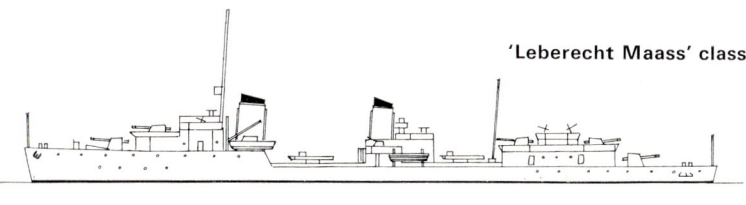

'Leberecht Maass' class

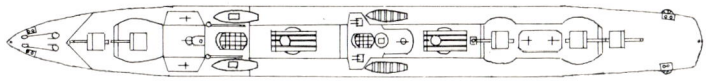

'Leberecht Maass' class (16 ships)

**Z1 (LEBERECHT MAASS), Z2 (GEORG THIELE)*,
Z3 (MAX SCHULTZ), Z4 (RICHARD BEITZEN),
Z5 (PAUL JACOBI), Z6 (THEODOR RIEDEL),
Z7 (HERMAN SCHOEMANN), Z8 (BRUNO HEINEMANN),
Z9 (WOLFGANG ZENKER)*, Z10 (HANS LODY),
Z11 (BERNARD VON ARNIM)*, Z12 (ERICH GIESE)*,
Z13 (ERICH KOELLNER)*, Z14 (FRIEDRICH IHN),
Z15 (ERICH STEINBRINCK),
Z16 (FRIEDRICH ECKOLDT)**

Displacement: 2,200 tons.
Dimensions: 374 (OA) × 37.
Armament: 5 × 5 inch, 4 × 37mm, various 20mm, 8 torpedo tubes.
Speed: 38 knots, 70,000 SHP.
Complement: 315.   Built: 1937–39.

'Leberecht Maass' class   IWM-HU1050   1940

Leberecht Maass 1/1937

Theodor Riedel IWM 1942

'Von Roeder' class (6 ships)
**Z17 (DIETHER VON ROEDER)*,
Z18 (HANS LUDEMANN)*, Z19 (HERMANN KUNNE)*,
Z20 (KARL GALSTER), Z21 (WILHELM HEIDKAMP)*,
Z22 (ANTON SCHMITT)***

Displacement:	2,400 tons.
Dimensions:	384 (OA) × 38½.
Armament:	5 × 5 inch, 6 × 37 mm, various 20mm, 8 torpedo tubes.
Speed:	38 knots, 70,000 SHP.
Complement:	315. Built: 1938–39.

General Note: All the above classes were equipped for minelaying and could carry 60 mines. The single 5·9 inch guns could not be used for anti-aircraft purposes, due to low elevation; additional 37 mm and 20mm guns were fitted as the war progressed. The twin 5·9 inch guns in turrets were HA/LA with maximum elevation of about 60°.

Karl Galster IWM-HU3284 1940

Hans Ludemann　　　　　　　　　　　　　　　　1939

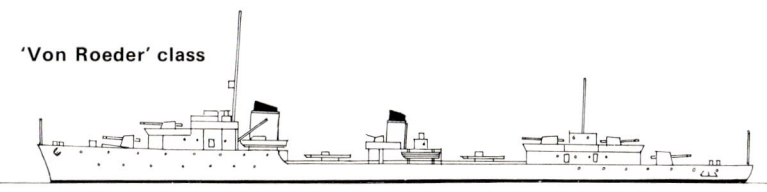

'Von Roeder' class

Leopard ('Wolf' class)　　　　　　　　　　　　　6/1937

'Möwe' class (6 ships)
AT (ALBATROSS), FK (FALKE), GR (GREIF), KO (KONDER), MO (MOWE), SE (SEEADLER)

Displacement:　924 tons.
Dimensions:　280 (OA) × $27\frac{1}{2}$.
Armament:　3 × 4·1 inch, 4 × 20mm, 6 torpedo tubes.
Speed:　32 knots, 23,000 SHP.
Complement:　130.　　　　　　　　　Built: 1926–28.

'Wolf' class (6 ships)
IT (ILTIS), JA (JAGUAR), LP (LEOPARD), LU (LUCHS), TG (TIGER), WL (WOLF)

Displacement:　933 tons.
Dimensions:　304 (OA) × 28.
Armament:　3 × 4·1 inch (**Leopard** and **Luchs** 3 × 5 inch), 4 × 20mm, 6 torpedo tubes.
Speed:　32 knots, 23,000 SHP.
Complement:　130.　　　　　　　　　Built: 1927–29.

Albatross ('Möwe' class)   IWM-HU1054   1940

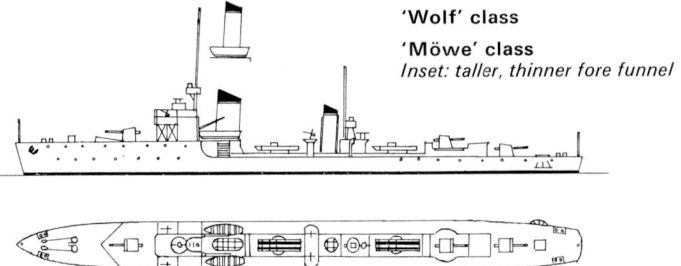

'Wolf' class
'Möwe' class
Inset: taller, thinner fore funnel

Iltis ('Wolf' class)   1938

'T1 to 'T21' class (21 ships)
No names, numbered 1 to 21 inclusive
Displacement: 840 tons (T9–T12), 844 tons (T1–T8), 853 tons (T13–T21).
Dimensions: 267 (OA) × 28.
Armament: 1 × 4·1 inch, 1 × 37mm, various 20mm, 6 torpedo tubes. Fitted for minelaying, 30 mines.
Speed: 35 knots, 31,000 SPH.   Built: 1938–42.

General Note: In these first three groups of torpedo boats some ships had one set of torpedo tubes removed and a 40mm gun substituted. Additional 20mm guns were added later.

Two of the early 'T' series torpedo boats at speed in the Baltic in the summer of 1943. The basic hull colour is a very light grey with extra dark grey camouflage patches; the entire bow is painted this colour also. The ship illustrated below is painted in a similar style.

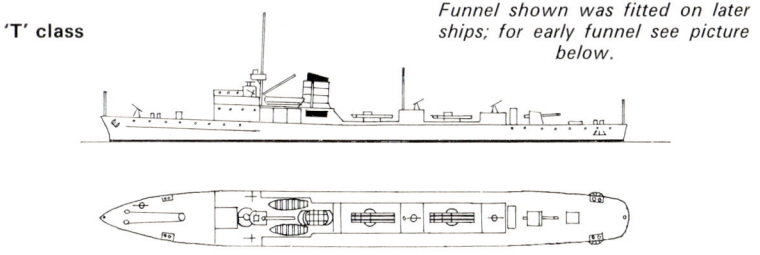

'T' class

Funnel shown was fitted on later ships; for early funnel see picture below.

Early 'T' class   IWM-HU1046   1942

'T22' to 'T36' class (15 ships)
No names, numbered 22 to 36 inclusive

Displacement: 1,294 tons.
Dimensions: 315 (OA) × 31.
Armament: 4 × 4·1 inch, 4 × 37mm, various 20mm, 6 torpedo tubes.
Speed: 33 knots, 32,000 SHP.
Complement: 200.

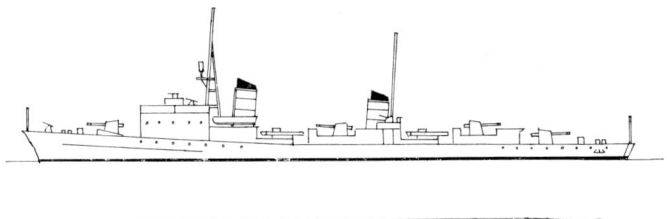

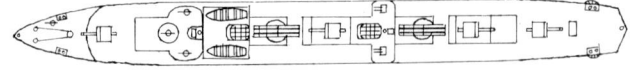

T33   1945

BELOW: The Arcena *was an old light cruiser stripped down and converted to an anti-aircraft ship for harbour defence. It had a battery of Flak 18 AA guns and smaller calibres (IWM-HU3299).*

Type IIA (U2) 1/1937

Submarines

SPACE precludes mention of every submarine, especially the many experimental types, but included are all the main operational types with data and their numbers, which were all prefixed with the letter U'. The first figures in tonnage and speed refer to the surface and the second to submerged conditions. After all the data tables is a separate section covering the 'U' numbers of the different types. Only one type of midget submarine was really significant—the XXVIIB **'Seehund'**—as the others, some of which are illustrated in the photographs, were little more than human torpedoes. They had only a small radius of action and had to be transported by road or rail to almost their point of operations. With Allied air power covering all transport routes this proved to be almost a physical impossibility and, in any case, their development had been left far too late in the war for them to be effective. Types included **'Neger'**, **'Marder'**, **'Biber'** and **'Molch'**, and it is worth noting that over 1,200 were built; had they been developed earlier in the war there is little doubt that they could have caused serious losses to the Allied invasion ships.

Type II, 'A', 'B', 'C', 'D' (coastal type)

Displacement:	'A' 254/303 tons, 'B' 279/329 tons, 'C' 291/341 tons, 'D' 314/364 tons.
Dimensions:	'A' 134 (OA) × 13, 'B' 140 (OA) × 13, 'C' 143 (OA) × 13½, 'D' 144 (OA) × 16.
Armament:	3 torpedo tubes, 1 or 4 × 20mm, 8 mines.
Speed:	'A' 13/7 knots, 'B' 13/7 knots, 'C' 12/7 knots, 'D' 13¾/7 knots.
Maximum range:	'A' 1,050, 'B' 1,800, 'C' 1,900, 'D' 3,500 nautical miles.
Complement:	25. Built: 1935–40.

Type IIA — 1/1937

Type II
(A, B, C, D)

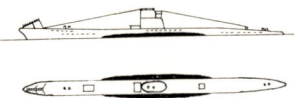

Type XIII was similar but slightly larger.

Type IIB (U9) — IWM-HU1012 — 1938

Type IIB — 4/1940

Type I (U25 and U26—2 boats) (ocean type)

Displacement: 862/983 tons.
Dimensions: 237½ (OA) × 20¼.
Armament: 6 tubes, 1 × 4·1 inch and 1 × 20mm AA.
Speed: 18/8¼ knots.
Maximum range: 6,700 miles.
Complement: 43. Built: 1936.
  Note: Based on Turkish design; both sunk 1940.

The German Fleet at sea at the time of the Battle of the Barents Sea in 1943. The ship ahead is believed to be Admiral Hipper, *viewed from the deck of the* Lützow. *Note the yellow turret top, a recognition device for aircraft.*

Type I (U25)   4/1936

Type VII, 'A', 'B', 'C'

Displacement: 'A' 626/745 tons, 'B' 753/857 tons, 'C' 769/871 tons, 'C'(42) 999/1,050 tons.
Dimensions: 'A' 211 (OA) × 19, 'B' 218 (OA) × 20, 'C' 220 (OA) ×20, 'C'(42) 225 (OA) × 22.
Armament: 5 torpedo tubes, 1 × 3·5 inch, 'C' 1 × 37mm, others 20mm.
Speed: 'A' 16/8 knots, 'B' $17\frac{1}{4}/8$ knots, 'C' $17/17\frac{1}{2}$ knots, 'C' (42) $16\frac{3}{4}/7\frac{1}{2}$ knots.
Maximum range: 'A' 4,300, 'B' and 'C' 6,500. 'C'(42) 10,000, Type XIV 9,300 nautical miles.
Complement: 'A', 'B', 'C' 44, 'C'(42) 45, Type XIV 53. Built: 1936–44.
  'C'(42) refers to a slightly enlarged version, made in 1942, with longer range and the hull was strengthened for deeper submerged operations. Type XIV similar but no torpedo tubes.

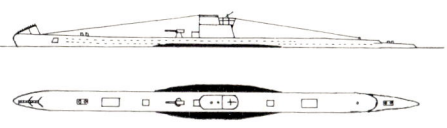

Type VII (A, B, C)

Type XIV similar but no torpedo tubes — used as tankers.

47

Type VIIA (U32) IWM-HU1011 1938

Type VIIA (AA gun on after casing) 9/1938

Type VIIA 10/1939

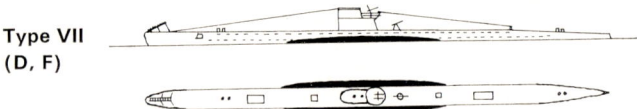

Type VII (D, F)

Type VII, 'D' and 'F'

Displacement: 'D' 965/1,080 tons, 'F' 1,084/1,181 tons.
Dimensions: 'D' 252 (OA) × 21, 'F' 254 (OA) × 24.
Armament: 5 torpedo tubes, 1 × 37mm, 2 × 20mm.
Speed: 'D' 16/7$\frac{1}{4}$ knots, 'F' 17/8 knots.
Maximum range: 'D' 10,000 'F' 9,500 nautical miles.
Complement: 44.   Built: 1942–43.

The 'D' was an improved and larger version of 'A', 'B' and 'C' types. The 'F' version was a torpedo transport, for operational boats, and carried 25 extra torpedoes.

Type VIIB (rendezvous scene in Atlantic)   *9/1941*

Type VIIC (U570 after capture)   8/1942

Type VIIA (U35)   10/1939

Type IX, 'A', 'B', 'C'
Displacement: 'A' 1,032/1,153 tons, 'B' 1,051/1,178 tons, 'C' 1,120/1,232 tons.
Dimensions: 252 (OA) × 22.
Armament: 6 torpedo tubes, 1 × 4·1 inch, 1 × 37mm, 1 × 20mm.
Speed: 18/7 knots.
Maximum range: 'A' 8,100, 'B' 8,700, 'C' 11,000 nautical miles.
Complement: 48.   Built: 1940–43.

These were long-range boats developed from Type IA.

Type IX
(A, B, C)

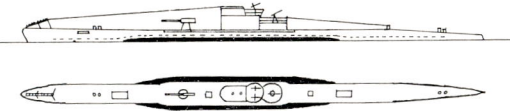

Type VIIB   *5/1940*

Type IX, 'D1', 'D2'

Displacement: 'D1' 1,610/1,799 tons, 'D2' 1,616/1,804 tons.
Dimensions: $287\frac{1}{2}$ (OA) × $24\frac{1}{2}$.
Armament: 'D2' 6 torpedo tubes ('D1' nil), 1 × 4·1 inch ('D1' nil), 37 and 20mm.
Speed: 'D1' 16/7 knots, 'D2' $19\frac{1}{4}/7$ knots.
Maximum range: 'D1' 9,900, 'D2' 23,700 nautical miles.
Complement: 57.   Built: 1942–44.
'D1's were tankers; 'D2's were exceptionally long-range boats.

No forward gun on 'D1'

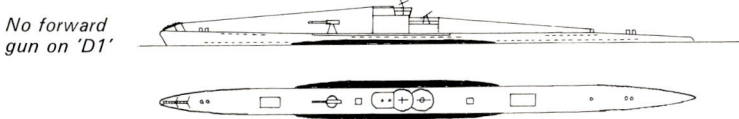

Type XII of same external appearance and size.

Type IX D1 and D2 (background with gun)   *1/1944*

51

Type VIIA   *1940*

Type XB

Displacement: 1,763/2,177 tons.
Dimensions: 295 (OA) × 30.
Armament: 2 torpedo tubes, 1 × 4·1 inch, 1 × 37mm, 1 × 20mm, 66 mines.
Speed: 16½/7 knots.
Maximum range: 14,450 nautical miles.
Complement: 52.

    These were the largest submarines used by Germany. Used frequently as supply boats although designed originally as minelayers.

Type XA

    Forerunner of Type XB, slightly longer, with mines carried externally.

Type XB

Type XA similar

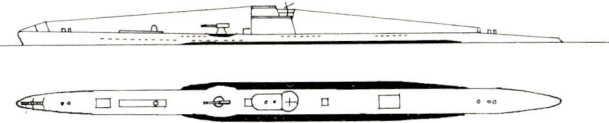

Type XII

Externally similar to Type IX but with more powerful engines and two extra torpedo tubes (8 in all).

Type XIII

This was a war-built version of the Type II, slightly increased in displacement (400 tons) and with a higher speed of 15 knots. It was otherwise similar to the Type II.

Type XIII *1945*

Type XIV

Submarine tankers generally similar in size and appearance to Type VIIA. See page 47. These boats supported operational vessels, supplying fuel and replacement torpedoes. Built in small numbers.

Type XVII 'A', 'B', 'G'

Small coastal types similar in size to the Type II and Type XIII boats but with a more streamlined hull and lower conning tower; no guns. These were built mainly to test the Walter HTP (peroxide-fuelled) turbine engine in a small production series.

Type XVIII

Ocean type scheduled to have Walter HTP turbines, the two initial vessels were abandoned before completion.

Type XXI

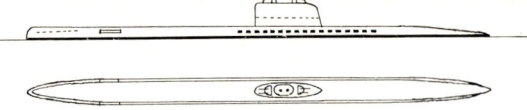

Type XXI
Displacement: 1,612/1,819 tons.
Dimensions: 251 (OA) × 22.
Armament: 6 torpedo tubes, 4 × 30mm.
Speed: $15\frac{1}{2}$/16 knots.
Maximum range: 11,150 nautical miles.
Complement: 57.

Fully streamlined hull; long range boats capable of fully submerged operations.

Type XXIII
Displacement: 232/256 tons.
Dimensions: 112 (OA) × 10.
Armament: 2 torpedo tubes.
Speed: $9\frac{3}{4}$/$12\frac{1}{2}$ knots.
Maximum range: 1,350 nautical miles.
Complement: 14.

These were coastal versions of the type XXI for short range operations.

The Biber *(Beaver) class was one of the most numerous of the midget submarines, a total of 324 being built. It had a one-man crew and carried a 21 inch torpedo slung each side of the lower hull in the shaped recess. This class was $29\frac{1}{2}$ feet long and displaced 63 tons. Speed 6 knots.*

Type XXVIIB 'Seehund'

Displacement: 15 tons.
Dimensions: 39 (OA) × 5½.
Armament: 2 torpedoes carried externally.
Speed: 7¼/6 knots.
Maximum range: 500 nautical miles.
Complement: 2.

These were the most successful of the midget submarines but were developed too late in the war to be really effective.

LEFT: The Molch *class midget submarine also carried two torpedoes externally in shaped hull recesses. About 390 vessels were built. Length 35½ feet, speed 5 knots, and crew one. RIGHT: A* Seehund *class midget submarine showing torpedo stowage.*

SUBMARINE NUMBERS

Type 1 'A' (2 boats)
25 and 26.
Type II 'A' to 'D' (50 boats)
1–24, 56–63, 120–121, 137–152.
Type VII 'A' to 'F' (723 boats)
27–32, 45–55, 69–82, 83–102, 132–136, 201–218, 221–232, 235–486, 551–683, 702–779, 821–822, 825–828, 901, 903–905, 907, 921–930, 951–995, 997–1010, 1013–1031, 1051–1065, 1101–1110, 1131–1132, 1161–1172, 1191–1210, 1271–1279, 1301–1308.
Type IX 'A' to 'C' (146 boats)
37–44, 64–68, 103–111, 122–131, 153–176, 183–194, 501–550, 801–806, 841–846, 853–858, 865–870, 877–881, 889.
Type IX 'D1' and 'D2' (49 boats)
177–182, 195–200, 847–852, 859–864, 871–876, 883, 1221–1238.
Type XB (8 boats)
116–119, 219–220, 233–234.
Type XIV (4 boats)
487–490.
Type XXI (126 boats)
2501–2552, 3001–3034, 3035, 3037–3041, 3044, 3047–3051, 3502–3530.
Type XXIII (51 boats)
2321–2371.

Aircraft Carriers and Tenders

JUST before World War 2 and up till 1942 there were some interesting projects which—had they come about—might have considerably influenced the course of naval operations. In December 1938 the large, for that time, aircraft carrier **Graf Zeppelin** was launched at Kiel and the keel of her sister ship **Peter Strasser** was laid down shortly after. Later in the war, as emergency measures, it was also visualized that the liners **Europa, Gneisenau** and **Potsdam** plus the heavy cruiser **Seydlitz** could be converted into aircraft carriers. However, these plans were never carried out; by 1942 all work had stopped on the **Graf Zeppelin** hull, and the **Peter Strasser** was scrapped on the stocks. The last remaining relic of these ships, the incompleted hull of the **Graf Zeppelin**, was towed to Leningrad after the war and broken up in 1948. Junkers 87 dive bombers and Me 109 fighters were envisaged for operation from these carriers.

If the **Bismarck** had been able to sail with a large fast aircraft carrier in company, then the outcome of her forlorn sortie might have been vastly different. Shadowing British aircraft would have been driven off, or shot down, and the attacking torpedo bombers—whose hits sealed her fate—would have stood little chance of getting within effective range. Then, with the open Atlantic to operate in, the two ships could have wreaked havoc amongst the convoys which were the life line of Britain. The success of such a mission might easily have led to other sorties by **Tirpitz, Scharnhorst** and **Gneisenau**, which would have constituted a serious menace to Britain at this stage of the war when she stood alone. Engagements would have been fought, in the style of Midway a year later, with the aircraft carriers as principal targets for the naval aircraft from their opposite numbers. Bearing in mind the large number of British warships required to hunt down the **Bismarck** then it is not hard to visualize, if German carrier task forces had been formed, that the resources of the Royal Navy would have been stretched to the limit to combat this menace.

Unlike the other major sea powers in World War 2, Great Britain, U.S.A. and Japan, German naval aviation never developed enough to play an active rôle. The only aircraft ever to go to sea, in the true sense, were those carried by the few large warships and armed raiders that made long range sorties against merchant shipping. These were Arado two-seater seaplanes, manned by

GRAF ZEPPELIN

Displacement:	23,200 tons.
Dimensions:	820 × 88½ × 18½.
Armament:	16 × 5·9 inch,
	12 × 4·1 inch,
	22 × 37mm.
Speed:	33½ knots
	(200,000 HP).
Maximum range:	8,000 miles
	(19 knots)
Complement:	1,760.

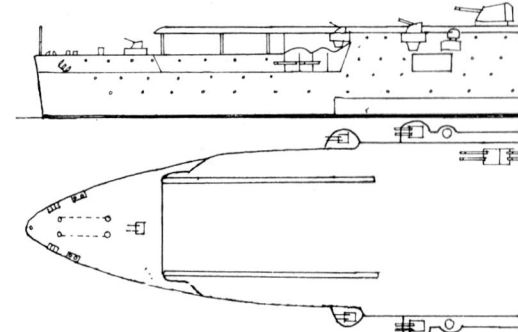

"FRIESENLAND"
(Catapult Ship)

"SCHWABENLAND"
(Catapult Ship)

"WESTFALEN"

Luftwaffe personnel, launched by catapult and recovered from the sea by crane. A few reconnaissance sorties were made from the pocket battleships and armed raiders and, in this aspect, some measure of success was achieved with the spotting of stray merchant ships. During the Norwegian campaign some reconnaissance missions by large flying boats, operated from pre-war special merchant ships, but were not of great significance.

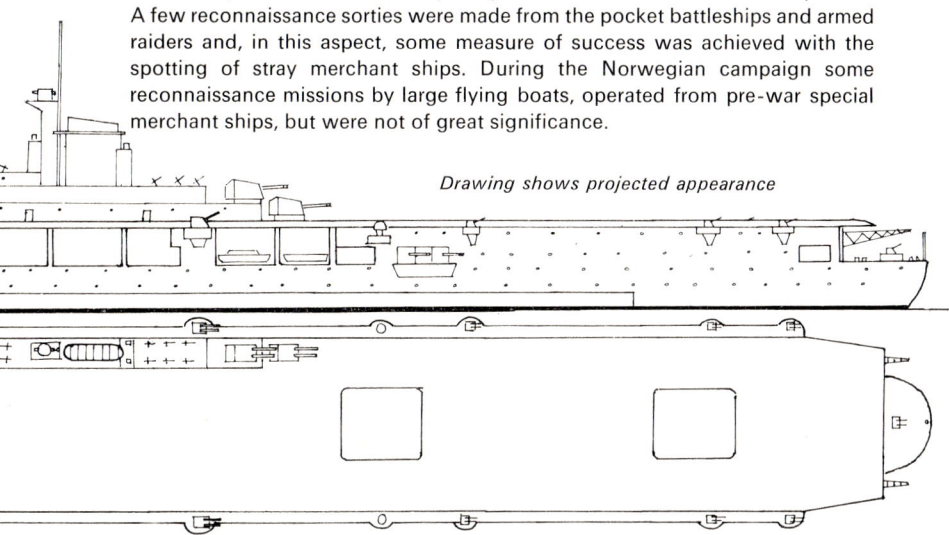

Drawing shows projected appearance

Friesenland   1939

FRIESENLAND
Displacement: 5,434 tons.   *Side view drawings,*
Length: 455¼ ft.   *page 57.*
Speed: 16 knots.

SCHWABENLAND
Displacement: 8,188 tons.
Length: 468 ft.
Speed: 12 knots.

Schwabenland   1936

Westfalen   *1936*

WESTFALEN   Displacement: 5,365 tons.
                     Length: 409 ft.
                     Speed: 11·5 knots.

Ostmark   *1940*

OSTMARK   Displacement: 1,200 tons.
                   Length: 242 ⅔ ft.
                   Speed: 13·5 knots.

Before the war the large liner **Bremen** carried her own catapult, positioned between the two funnels, and a seaplane was launched a day before the ship was due in port. Consequently the mail, carried by the seaplane, took a day less to deliver. Extending this idea, three catapult-equipped merchant ships—**Friesenland, Schwäbenland** and **Westfalen**—formed a chain across the Atlantic to quicken the delivery of mail. However, with the advent of longer ranged and more reliable flying boats and aircraft this idea was already outmoded before World War 2. During the war these three ships were used in the Norwegian campaign, manned by Merchant Service crews and with associated Luftwaffe air personnel. They operated a small number of reconnaissance missions. After their brief spell of operations these rather awkward ships, which were comparatively slow and large, were sent to the Baltic where they saw very little service. A smaller ship, completed before the war for the same rôle, the **Ostmark** also operated in the Baltic.

Some smaller, faster and more practical aircraft tenders were built during the war, including the following: **Walter Holtzapfel, Immelmann, Max Stinsky** and **Falke.** Their main feature was a large mobile crane which ran on rails over the after half of the ship. Originally the intention was for the crane to lift a large flying boat out of the water and then, after moving a long way forward, to place it on the after deck which was completely clear. However, with this unique feature, they were readily adaptable for other auxiliary tasks, the most important of which was salvage. All survived the war.

Grief   1939

GRIEF
Displacement: 960 tons.
Armament: 1 × 4·1 inch.
Length: 236¼ ft.
Speed: 19 knots.   Built: 1936.

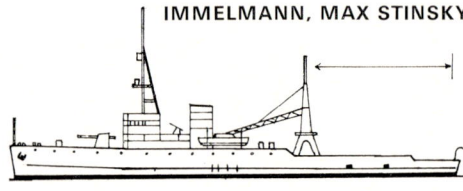
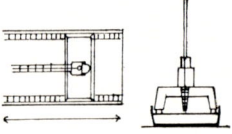

Crane detail

IMMELMANN, MAX STINSKY
Displacement: 1,000 tons.
Length: 246 ft.
Armament: 1 × 4·1 inch, 2 × 20mm.
Speed: 20·5 knots.   Built: 1941.

These ships were slightly enlarged versions of **Grief**, similar in appearance but with a less prominent aircraft crane jib mounted in a higher tower. These ships were acquired by France in 1945.

Krischau I   1940

KRISCHAU I
Displacement: 200 tons.   Small harbour type of seaplane tender.
Length: 121½ ft.
Speed: 15 knots.

Walter Holzapfel   Real Photographs   1942

WALTER HOLZAPFEL

Displacement: 1,200 tons.
Dimensions: 260 × 38.
Speed: 17 knots.
Complement: 61.   Built: 1940.

This ship was acquired by the Royal Navy in 1945 and became a diving tender, renamed **Deepwater**.

1940 appearance shown —radar later fitted, as in photograph above.

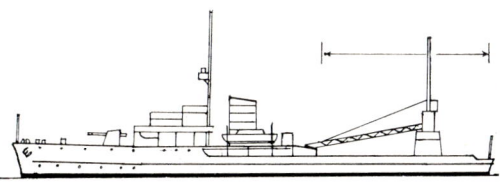

WALTER HOLZAPFEL

FALKE

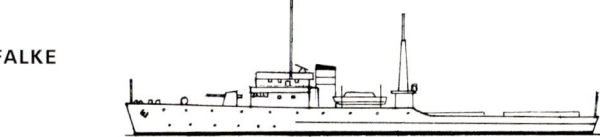

FALKE (ex-GUNTER PLUSCHOW)

Displacement: 1,000 tons.
Dimensions: 256 × 36.
Armament: 1 × 4·1 inch plus light AA.
Speed: 23 knots.

This ship was acquired by the USSR after the war and was renamed **Kodor**.

Minesweepers

ALL minesweepers had the prefix letter M, and the type number referred to the year of design, eg, 43 = 1943.

Type M43

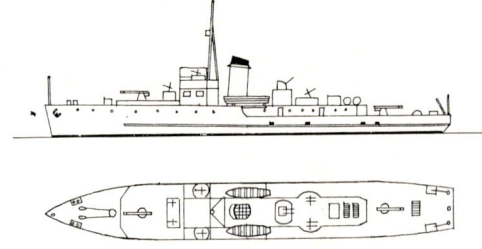

Type M43 (20 ships)
Numbers: 601–612, 801–808.

Displacement:	605 tons.
Dimensions:	222 (OA) × 29.
Armament:	2 × 4·1 inch, 2 × 37mm, plus 20mm. (Some fitted to carry mines.)
Speed:	16½ knots.
Complement:	107.

Type M40 (131 ships)
Numbers: 261–267, 271–279, 291–294, 301–307, 321–330, 341–348, 361–377, 381–389, 401–408, 411–416, 421–428, 431–438, 441–446, 451–456, 459–463, 467–471, 475–476, 483–484, 486, 489, 495–496.

Displacement:	543 tons.
Dimensions:	197 (OA) × 28.
Armament:	2 × 4·1 inch, 1 × 37mm, plus 20mm.
Speed:	17 knots.
Complement:	76.

M40

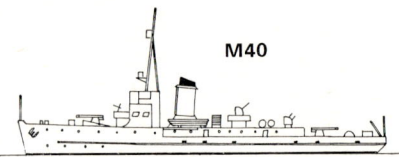

M35

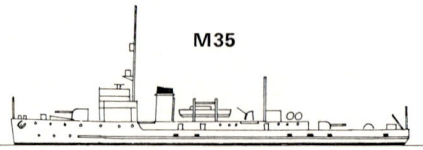

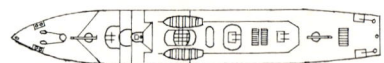

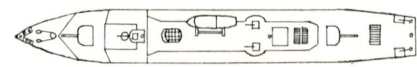

Type M35

Type M35 (69 ships)
Numbers: 1–39, 81–85, 101–107, 131–133, 151–156, 201–206, 251–256.

Displacement: 717 tons.
Dimensions: 216 (OA) × 27.
Armament: 2 × 4·1 inch, 2 × 37mm, plus 20mm. (Some fitted to carry mines.)
Complement: 10.

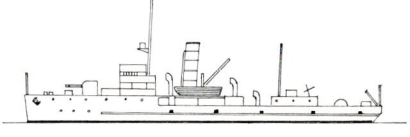

Type M1915

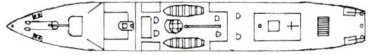

Type M1915 (36 ships)
Numbers: 61, 85, 89, 132, 502, 504, 507–511, 513, 515, 517, 522, 526, 528–530, 533–536, 538, 545, 546, 550, 557, 560, 566, 572, 575, 581, 582, 584, 598.

Displacement: 525 tons.
Dimensions: 192 (OA) × 24.
Armament: 1 × 4·1 inch, plus 20mm.
Speed: 16 knots.
Complement: 50.

Ex World War 1 ships. Apart from above numbers there were several others used for general duty work and tenders (see page 83).

Type M1915 (converted to harbour tender)   1945

Escort Vessels

F2   IWM-HU1002   4/1938

F1 to F10 (10 ships)
Displacement: 712 tons.
Dimensions: 241 (OA) × 29.
Armament: 2 × 4·1 inch, 4 × 37mm, plus 20mm.
Speed: 28 knots, 14,000 SHP.
Complement: 121.   Built: 1936–38.

'F' class

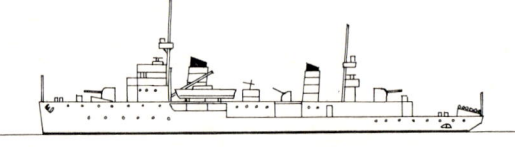

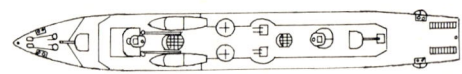

BRUMMER 1
Displacement: 2,410 tons.
Dimensions: 354 (OA) × 44.
Armament: 4 × 4·1 inch, 2 × 3·5 inch, 4 × 37mm, 450 mines.
Speed: 20 knots, 8,000 SHP.
Complement: 182.   Built: 1925.
Gunnery training and minelayer. Sunk in Norwegian campaign, 1940.

BRUMMER I   Topmast not shown

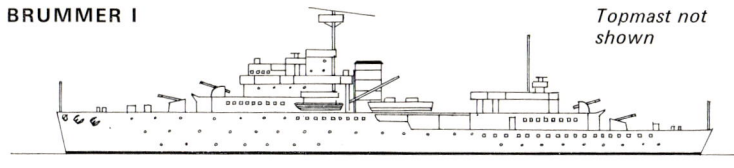

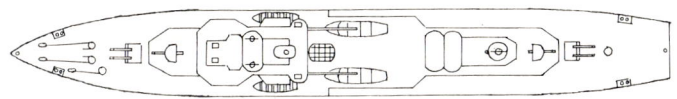

Bremse   1941

BREMSE

Displacement: 1,460 tons.
Dimensions: 318 (OA) × 31.
Speed: 27 knots, Diesels.
Complement: 192.   Built: 1931.
Gunnery training and minelayer. Sunk by British cruisers in Russian convoy action, 1941.

BREMSE

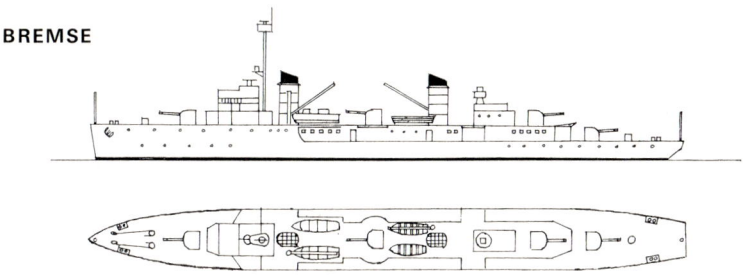

K3

Displacement: 1,365 tons.   Complement: 156.
Dimensions: 247 × 33½.
Speed: 15 knots.
Armament: 4 × 4·7 inch, 4 × 20mm.   Built: 1941–42.
Built in Rotterdam using Dutch material. Large patrol vessel or gunboat. Taken over by Dutch Navy in 1945.

K3 (see previous page)   1942

'E' Boats

Motor torpedo boats, known in Germany as 'S' boats. Usually armed with two fixed torpedo tubes forward, plus 1 × 40mm or 1 × 37mm, plus 20mm. Sizes: 50–100 tons, 90–115 ft, all capable of high speed (35–42 knots). Larger types could carry 6–8 mines.

S700 series: building 1945.
S200/S300 series: building 1944–45.
S170/S186/S195 series: built 1944.
S151 series: built 1943.
S100 to S190 series: built 1943–44.
S38 to S100 series: built 1942–43.
S20 to S60 series: built 1940–41.
Earlier numbers: built 1934–39.

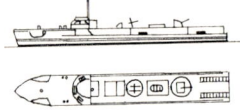

'E' Boat ('S' Boat) S195 series   6/1945

'E' Boat ('S' Boat) S195 series 5/1945

'R' Boats

Large coastal motor launches used for a variety of duties which included minesweeping, minelaying, convoy escort and general duties. Usually armed with 1 × 37mm plus 20mm, depth charges or mines. Varying sizes: 60–150 tons, 85–135 ft. Medium speeds: 17–21 knots.

R400 series: building 1944–45.
R200 to R300 series: building 1944–45.
R150 to R200 series: built 1943.
R130 to R150: built 1943.
R41 to R129 series: built 1943.
R25 to R40 series: built 1938.
R17 to R24 series: built 1937.
R1 to R17 series: built 1934–36.

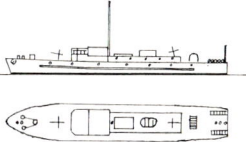

R28 (typical 'R' Boat) 1942

Patrol Trawlers

Like Britain, Germany used many trawlers for such duties as minesweeping and convoy escort. A typical type was approximately 500 tons, 120 ft, and armed with 1 × 3·5 inch, plus 20mm or machine guns, plus depth charges.

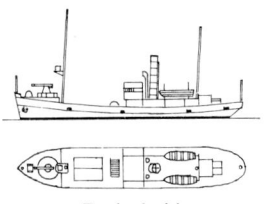

Typical older type trawler.

Koningsau (typical trawler)

Landing Craft

THE following types were purpose-built in 1940. There were also many converted commercial barges.

Siebel Ferry   1940

Siebel Ferry
Dimensions: 75 × 56.
Armament: 3 × 8·8cm, 2 × 20mm.
Twin hull vessel driven by aero engines.
Prominent rangefinder on bridge.

'F' Boat
Capacity: 120 tons.
Armament: MGs.
Purpose-built flat bottom barge with ramp.

'F' Boat   1940

Depot and Supply Ships

Saar 1/1937

DEPOT SHIPS

SAAR (Submarines)

Displacement: 2,710 tons.
Dimensions: 308 (OA) × 44.
Armament: 3 × 4·1 inch plus 20mm.
Speed: 16 knots, Diesels.
Complement: 214.   Built: 1934.

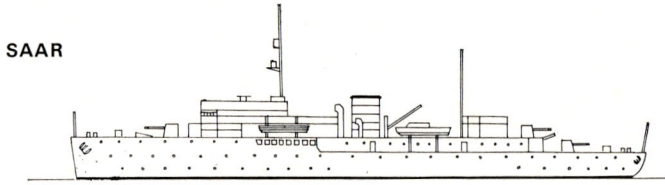

SAAR

WILHELM BAUER, WALDEMAR KOPHAMEL (Submarines)
ADOLF LUDERITZE ('E' Boats)

Displacement: 3,615 tons.
Dimensions: 374 × 47½.
Armament: 2 × 4·1 inch plus small AA.
Speed: 20 knots.   Built: 1939–40.

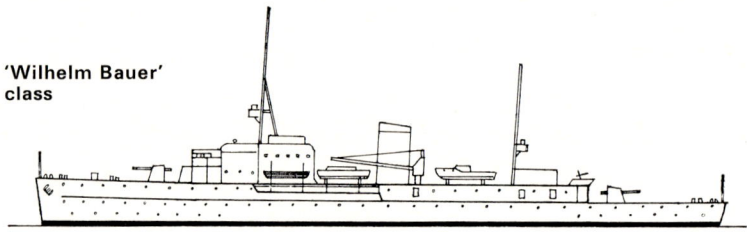

'Wilhelm Bauer' class

WEICHSEL, DONAU (Submarines)

Displacement: 3,974 and 3,886 tons.
Dimensions: 309 × 44 and 287 × 41.
Armament: 1 × 4·1 inch plus small AA.
Speed: 10 knots.
Note: The second set of figures apply to **Donau** which was slightly smaller and had a different bow shape (see drawing). Both were merchant ships, built 1922–23, and converted to their naval rôle in 1936–37. After the war the **Weichsel** was acquired by USSR.

Donau *bow detail.*

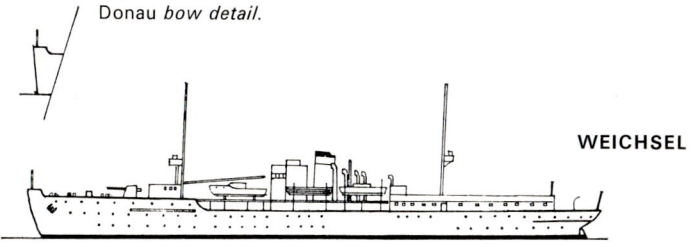

WEICHSEL

ERWIN WASSNER (Submarines)
Displacement: 5,000 tons (approx).
Dimensions: 380 × 55.
Armament: Light AA.
Speed: 15 knots (approx).
Note: Completed in 1938 as a cargo ship, it was immediately taken over by the Navy as a depot ship for the expanding submarine programme.

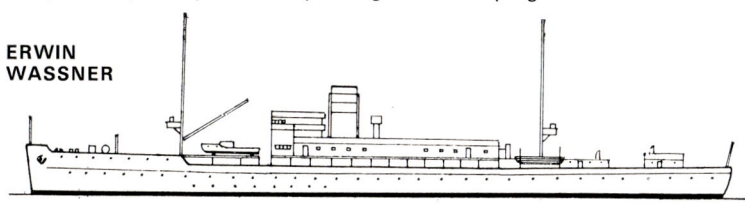

ERWIN WASSNER

ISAR, LECH (Submarines)
Displacement: 3,850 tons.
Dimensions: 319 × 45.
Armament: Light AA.
Speed: 12 knots.
Note: Both completed as cargo ships in 1930 and, in 1938, were converted to their wartime rôle. After the war the **Isar** was acquired by USSR.

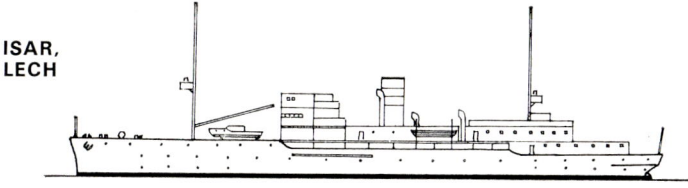

ISAR, LECH

LORELEI (ex-K4) (Submarines)
Displacement: 2,270 tons.
Dimensions: 323 × 34½.
Armament: 3 × 4·1 inch plus small AA.
Speed: 30 knots.

Drawing on next page

Note: Laid down by Belgium in 1939 and in 1940, after being taken over, was towed to Germany and completed as a submarine depot ship. When the war ended she was re-acquired by Belgium and renamed the **Artevelde**.

Hermann von Wissmann (in Belgian service, post-war)

HERMANN VON WISSMANN (Submarines)
Displacement: 3,840 tons.
Dimensions: 374 × 49¼.
Armament: Small AA.   Speed: 15 knots.   Built: 1940.
Ex-Polish ship completed for German Navy. Acquired post-war by Belgium and renamed **Artvelde**.

LORELEI

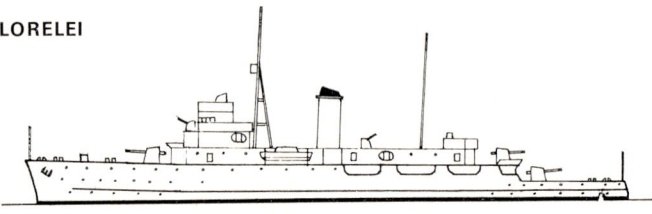

Smaller submarine depot ships
There were at least three smaller ships, less than 1,000 tons, used for this rôle and these included: **Memel** (998 tons, built 1937), **Mosel** (796 tons, built 1921), **Warnow** (726 tons, built 1906). In addition some of the numerous ex-World War 1 minesweepers converted into tenders were also earmarked for the submarine support rôle.

TSINGTAU

TANGA
(inset)

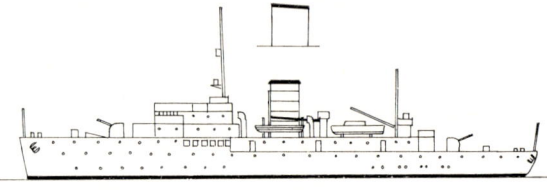

TSINGTAU ('E' and 'R' Boats)
TANGA
Displacement: 1,970 tons.
Dimensions: 279 (OA) × 44.
Armament: 2 × 3·5 inch plus 20mm.
Speed: 17½ knots, Diesels.
Complement: 134.   Built: 1934 and 1938.

STRAHL

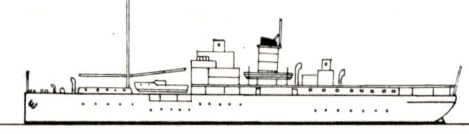

STRAHL (Tenders)
Displacement: 1,643 tons.
Dimensions: 235 × 33½.
Armament: Light AA.
Speed: 10 knots.
Note: An old converted merchant ship, built 1902, which was used as a general repair and maintenance ship for the many tenders that were in service.

Hela   IWM-HU3283   1940

HELA ('E' and 'R' Boats)
Displacement: 2,300 tons.
Dimensions: 323 × 42½.
Armament: 2 × 4·1 inch, 1 × 37mm, 2 × 20mm.
Speed: 18 knots.   Built: 1939.

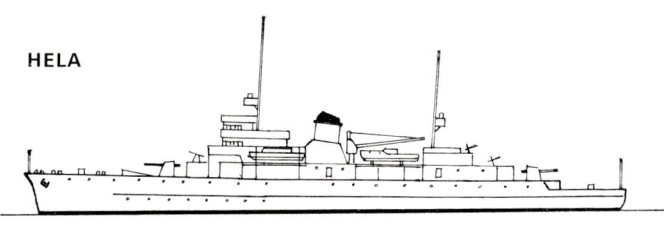

HELA

ELBE, WESER (Small ships and fishery protection)
Displacement: 1,600 tons.
Dimensions: 189 × 27¼.
Armament: 1 × 3·5 inch plus small AA.
Speed: 15 knots.   Built: 1931

WESER, ELBE

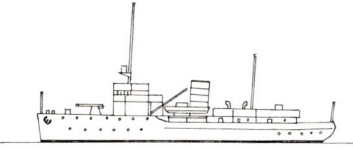

Nordmark (as HMS Bulawayo)   1945

SUPPLY SHIPS

NORDMARK, ALTMARK, DITT MARSCHEN, ERMLAND, FRANKEN

Displacement: 15,000 tons.
Dimensions: 582 × 72.
Speed: 21 knots.
Complement: 300 (approx).   Built: 1938–39.

These were used as replenishment ships for the major battle units, and were fast and well equipped.

KÄRTEN

Displacement: 5,660 gross tons.
Armament: 1 × 4·1 inch, 4 × 20 mm.
Speed: 16 knots.

Similar to **Altmark** class but slightly smaller in size and with no top masts. Acquired by USSR in 1945.

'Altmark' class

Note: **Altmark** was supply ship to **Graf Spee** in 1939. **Nordmark** served in Royal Navy post-war as **Bulawayo**.

Captured Ships

IT is not generally known that Germany took over and used many foreign warships from the countries that she occupied. Most of the captured ships came from Italy, they were lying in German occupied harbours, when that country capitulated on September 8, 1943. In all the Italian ships amounted to 7 destroyers, 29 torpedo boats and 25 submarines. Other countries included Norway: 1 minelayer, 2 destroyers, 4 torpedo boats and 2 submarines. France: 1 destroyer, 11 torpedo boats and 3 submarines. Holland: 1 destroyer and 5 submarines. Greece: 1 destroyer. Britain: 1 submarine. Many of these ships are illustrated and brief details of all are listed under their respective countries.

UB (ex-Seal) IWM-HU3274 1940

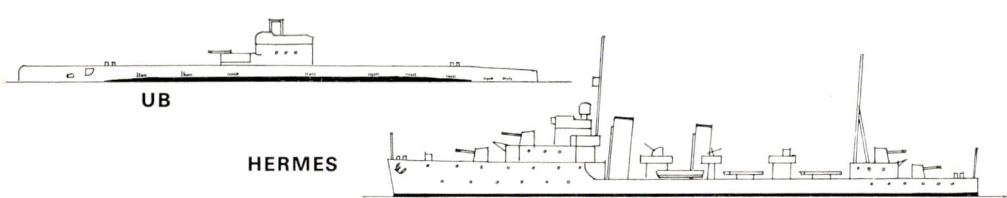

UB

HERMES

BRITAIN

Submarine
UB (SEAL)
1,520/2,157 tons; 289 (OA) × 25½; 6 × TT; 1 × 4 inch; 50 mines; 15/8¾ knots. Crew: 59.

GREECE

Destroyer
ZG 3, HERMES (VASILEVS GEORGIOS)
1,414 tons; 320 (OA) × 33; 4 × 5 inch; 4 × 37mm; 20mm; 8 × TT; 32 knots. Crew: 220.

HOLLAND

Destroyer
ZH 1 (GERARD CALLENBURGH)
1,628 tons; 384 (OA) × 34; 5 × 4·7 inch; 4 × 37mm; 20mm; 8 × TT; 37 knots. Crew: 236.
Submarines
UD 1 (0.8, H.6)
343/433 tons; 151 (OA) × 15; 1 × 37mm; 4 × TT; 13/8½ knots. Crew: 26.
UD 2 (O.12)
546/704 tons; 198 (OA) × 18; 2 × 40mm; 5 × TT; 15/8 knots. Crew: 31.
UD 3, 4 and 5 (O.25, 26 and 27)
881/1,380 tons; 225 (OA) × 22; 1 × 3·5 inch; 8 × TT; 19½/9 knots. Crew: 60.

UD 2   UD 3, UD 4, UD 5

NORWAY

Minelayer
BRUMMER 2, (ALBATROSS) (OLAVE TRYGGVASON)
1,596 tons; 304 (OA) × 37½; 4 × 5 inch; 2 × 37mm; 20mm; 280 mines; 20 knots. Crew: 168.
Destroyers
ZN 4, ZN 5 (TA 7 ex 1, TA 8 ex 2)
1,278 tons; 319 (OA) × 33; 4 × 4·7 inch; 2 × 37mm; 20mm; 4 × TT; 32 knots. Crew: 162.
Torpedo Boats
TIGER (TOR), PANTHER (ODIN), LEOPARD (BALDER), LOWE (GYLLER)
590 tons; 243 (OA) × 25½; 3 × 4 inch; 20mm; 4 × TT; 24 mines; 30 knots. Crew: 72.
Submarines
UC1 (B5), UC2 (B6)
420/545 tons; 167 (OA) × 17½; 1 × 3 inch; 4 × TT; 15/11 knots. Crew: 23.

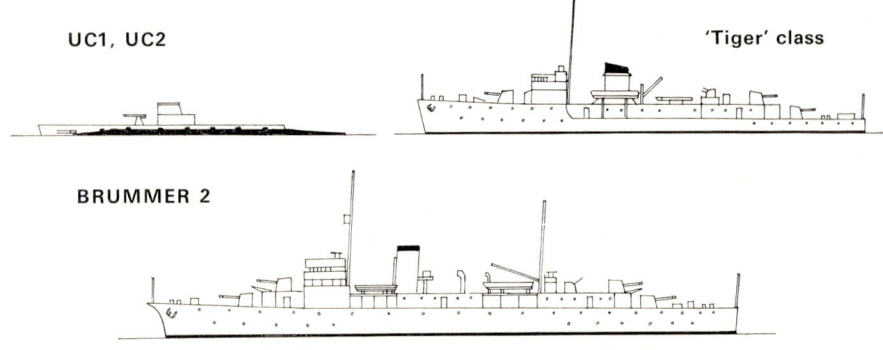

UC1, UC2   'Tiger' class

BRUMMER 2

UC1 4/1943

ZN 4, ZN 5

FRANCE

Destroyer
ZF 2 (L'OPINIATRE)
2,070 tons; 333 (OA) × 32½; 5 × 5 inch; 4 × 37mm; 20mm; 8 × TT; 37 knots. Crew: 245.

Torpedo Boats
TA1 (LE FIER), TA2 (L'AGILE), TA3 (L'ALSACIEN), TA4 (L'ENTREPRENANT), TA5 (LE FAROUCHE), TA6 (LE CORSE)
1,087 tons; 295 (OA) × 30½; 3 × 4·1 inch; 2 × 37mm; 20mm; 6 × TT; 33 knots. Crew: 147.

TA9 (FR42, BOMBARDE), TA10 (FR43, LA POMONE), TA11 (FR41, L'IPHIGENIE), TA12 (FR45, BALISTE), TA13 (FR44, LA BAYONNAISE)
610 tons; 245 (OA) × 26; 2 × 3·9 inch; 2 × 47mm; 20mm; 2 × TT; 34 knots. Crew: 92.

Submarines
UF1 (L'AFRICAINE), UF2 (LA FAVORITE), UF3 (L'ASTREE)
910/1,180 tons; 241 (OA) × 21; 1 × 3·5 inch; 10 × TT; 17/10 knots. Crew: 65.

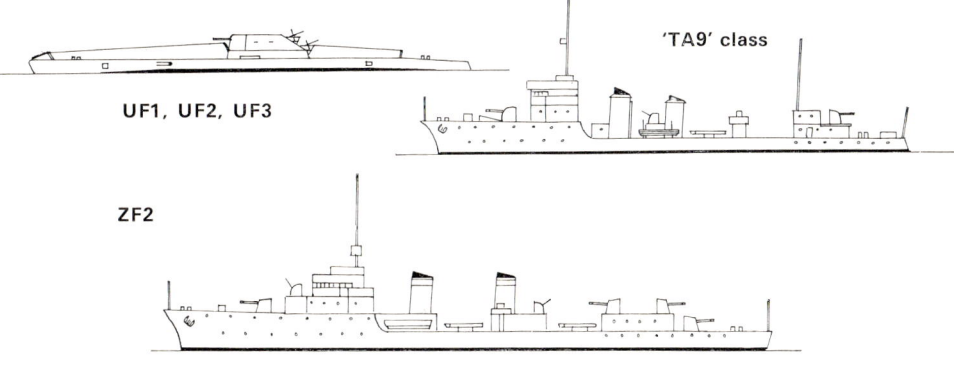

'TA9' class

UF1, UF2, UF3

ZF2

UA (ex-Batiray) 5/1941

TURKEY

Submarine
UA (BATIRAY)
1,044/1,357 tons; $282\frac{1}{4} \times 22\frac{1}{4}$; 1 × 4·1 inch; 1 × 20mm; 6 × TT and mines; 20/9 knots. Crew: 47.
German type building for Turkey but acquired by German Navy before completion.

ITALY

Destroyers
TA14 (Turbine)
1,092 tons; 300 (OA) × 30; 4 × 4·7 inch; 2 × 37mm; 20mm; 6 × TT 36 knots. Crew: 142.
TA32 (PREMUDA ex DUBROVNIK, Yugoslavia)
1,880 tons; 345 (OA) × 35; 4 × 5·5 inch; 2 × 3·4 inch; 6 × 40mm; 6 × TT; 31 knots. Crew: 200.
TA33 (CORSARO ex SQUADRISTA), TA34 (ARRISTA)
1,900 tons; 339 (OA) × 33; 5 × 4·7 inch; 20mm; 6 × TT; 50 mines; 38 knots. Crew: 207.
TZ43 (SEBENICO ex BEOGRAD, Yugoslavia)
1,210 tons; 313 (OA) × 31; 4 × 4·7 inch; 4 × 40mm; 6 × TT; 30 mines; 37 knots. Crew: 145.
TA44 (ANTONIA PIGAFETTA)
1,944 tons; 352 (OA) × 34; 6 × 4·7 inch; 2 × 37mm; 4 × TT; 52 mines; 39 knots. Crew: 170.
TA31 (DARDO)
1,206 tons; 302 (OA) × 32; 4 × 4·7 inch; 4 × 37mm; 20mm; 6 × TT; 38 knots. Crew: 126.

Torpedo Boats
TA15 (FRANCESCO CRISPI)
1,092 tons; 275 (OA) × 27; 4 × 4·7 inch; 2 × 37mm; 4 × TT; 36 knots. Crew: 120.
TA16 (CASTELFIDARDO), TA19 (CALATAFIMI)
966 tons; 262 (OA) × 24; 4 × 4 inch; 20mm; 6 × TT; 10 mines; 30 knots. Crew: 105.

TA17 (SAN MARTINO), TA18 (SOLFERINO)
862 tons; 256 (OA) × 24; 4 × 4 inch; 20mm; 4 × TT; 10 mines; 30 knots. Crew: 105.

TA20 (AUDACE ex KAWAKAZE, Japan)
629 tons; 275 (OA) × 25; 2 × 4 inch; 20mm; 4 × TT; 29 knots. Crew: 113.

TA21 (INSIDIO)
542 tons; 246 (OA) × 24; 2 × 4 inch; 20mm; 4 × TT; 29 knots. Crew: 105.

TA22 (GIUSEPPE MISSIRI), TA35 (GIUSEPPE DEZZA)
615 tons; 236 (OA) × 24; 2 × 4 inch; 20mm; 4 × TT; 30 knots. Crew: 105.

TA23 (IMPAVIDO), TA25 (INTREPIDO), TA26 (ARDITO)
1,204 tons; 275 (OA) × 31; 3 × 3·9 inch; 20mm; 4 × TT; 25 knots. Crew: 175.

TA48 (T3 ex 78T, Yugoslavia)
240 tons; 188 (OA) × 19; 2 × 66mm; 4 × TT; 28 knots. Crew: 52.

TA49 (LIRA)
799 tons; 255 (OA) × 26; 3 × 3·9 inch; 20mm; 4 × TT; 30 mines; 34 knots. Crew: 94.

TA24 (ARTURO), TA27 (AURIGA), TA28 (RIGEL), TA29 (ERIDANA), TA30 (DRAGONE), TA36 (STELLA POLARE), TA37 (GLADIO), TA38 (SPADA), TA39 (DAGA), TA40 (PUGNALE), TA41 (LANCIA), TA42 (ALABARDA), TA45 (SPICA), TA46 (FIONDA), TA47 (BALESTRA)
797 tons; 266 (OA) × 27; 2 × 3·9 inch; 4 × 37mm; 20mm; 6 × TT; 30 mines; $31\frac{1}{2}$ knots. Crew: 175.

Submarines

UIT.1 (R.10), UIT.2 (R.11), UIT.3 (R.12), UIT.4 (R.7), UIT.5 (R.8), UIT.6 (R.9)
1,300/2,600 tons; 285 (OA) × 25; no TT (cargo carriers); 20mm; 14/6 knots. Crew: 63.

UIT.7 (BARIO), UIT.8 (LITIO), UIT.9 (SODIO), UIT.10 (POTASSIO), UIT.11 (RAME), UIT. 12 (FERRO), UIT.13 (PIOMBO), UIT.14 (ZINCO)
928/1,131 tons; 211 (OA) × 23; 1 × 3·9 inch; 6 × TT; 16/8 knots. Crew: 59.

UIT.15 (SPARIDE), UIT.16 (MURENA), UIT.19 (NAUTILO), UIT.20 (GRONGO)
905/1,070 tons; 207 (OA) × 23; 1 × 3·9 inch; 6 × TT; 16/8 knots. Crew: 19.

UIT.17 (CM.1), UIT.18 (CM.2)
92/114 tons; 108 (OA) × 10; 2 × TT; 14/6 knots. Crew: 8.

UIT.21 (GIUSEPPE FINZI)
1,550/2,060 tons; 276 (OA) × 25; 2 × 4·7 inch; 8 × TT; 17/8 knots. Crew: 72.

UIT.22 (ALPINO BAGNOLINI), UIT.23 (REGINALDO GIULIANI)
1,166/1,484 tons; 250 (OA) × 23; 1 × 3·9 inch; 8 × TT; 18/8 knots. Crew: 57.

UIT.24 (COMMANDANTE CAPPELLINI)
1,060/1,313 tons; 240 (OA) × 24; 2 × 3·9 inch; 8 × TT; 17/8 knots. Crew: 57.

UIT.25 (LUIGI TORELLI)
1,191/1,489 tons; 250 (OA) × 22; 1 × 3·9 inch; 8 × TT; 18/8 knots. Crew: 57.

Auxiliary Cruisers

THESE were merchant ships specially converted to carry a concealed armament whose primary task was to destroy Allied merchant ships all over the world. Their secondary, and almost incidental, task was to tie down many warships in searching for them. In both tasks they were to succeed as will be shown by the brief details of the nine ships that actually sailed. Each ship was given a naval number prefixed by the letters HKS as well as a name, often chosen by her captain; original names are shown in brackets.

Note: TT: torpedo tubes. A/C: aircraft.

HSK 1, ORION (KURMARK) 1930
7,021 tons; 6 × 5·9 inch; 1 × 3 inch; 4 × 37mm; 20mm; 6 × TT; 2 × A/C; 230 mines.
Sunk or captured 9 ships (7 shared with **Komet**). Returned safely.

HSK 2, ATLANTIS (GOLDENFELS) 1937
7,860 tons; 6 × 5·9 inch; 1 × 3 inch; 2 × 37mm; 20mm; 4 × TT; 2 × A/C; 92 mines.
Sunk or captured 22 ships. Sunk by HMS **Devonshire,** November 23, 1941. Survivors reached home by German and Italian submarines.

HSK 3, WIDDER (NEUMARK) 1929
7,850 tons; 6 × 5·9 inch; 4 × 37mm; 20mm; 4 × TT; 2 × A/C; 60 mines.
Sunk or captured 10 ships. Returned safely.

HSK 4, THOR (SANTA CRUZ) 1938
3,860 tons; 6 × 5·9 inch; 2 × 37mm; 20mm; 4 × TT; 2 × A/C; 90 mines.
Sunk or captured 22 ships (two cruises). Accidently burnt out in Japan November 30, 1942.

HSK 5, PINGUIN (KANDELFELS) 1936
7,766 tons; 6 × 5·9 inch; 1 × 3 inch; 2 × 37mm; 20mm; 4 × TT; 2 × A/C; 300 mines.
Sunk or captured 28 ships. Sunk by HMS **Cornwall** May 8, 1941.

HSK 6, STIER (CAIRO) 1936
4,778 tons; 6 × 5·9 inch; 2 × 37mm; 20mm; 2 × TT; 2 × A/C.
Sunk or captured four ships. Sunk by merchant ship (USA **Stephen Hopkins** armed with only 1 × 4 inch) September 27, 1942.

HSK 7, KOMET (EMS) 1937
3,287 tons; 6 × 5·9 inch; 1 × 3 inch; 2 × 37mm; 6 × TT; 2 × A/C; 270 mines.
Sunk or captured 10 ships (7 shared with **Orion**). Sunk by British MTB October 14, 1942.

HSK 8, KORMORAN (STEIERMARK) 1938
8,736 tons; 6 × 5·9 inch; 4 × 37mm; 20mm; 4 × TT; 2 × A/C; 320 mines.
Sunk or captured 11 ships, plus HMAS **Sydney,** which also sank her December 11, 1942.

HSK 9, MICHEL (BIELSKO) 1939
4,740 tons; 6 × 5·9 inch; 3 × 37mm; 20mm; 4 × TT; 2 × A/C.
Sunk or captured 18 ships. Sunk by American submarine October 17, 1943.

Minor Vessels

SAIL TRAINING SHIPS

ALBERT LEO SCHLAGETER (1937)
HORST WESSEL (1936)
GORCH FOCK (1933) *

*Slightly smaller than above ships. Second figures in data table refer to this ship.

Displacement: 1,634 and 1,354 tons.
Dimensions: 295 (OA) × 39 and 242 (OA) × 39.
Armament: Machine guns.
Speed: 10 and 8 knots (under full sail faster), Diesels.
Complement: 289 and 255. Both figures include up to 200 cadets.

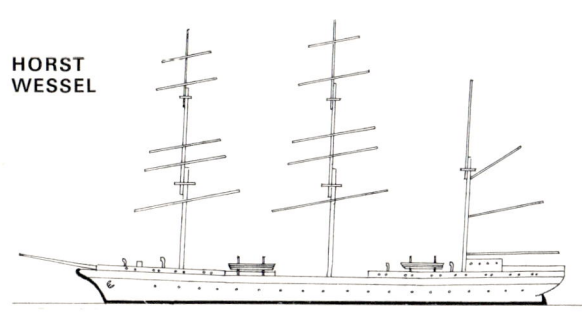

HORST WESSEL

SURVEY SHIPS

METEOR

Displacement: 1,200 tons.
Dimensions: 220 (OA) × 33.
Armament: 1 × 3·5 inch, plus 20mm.
Speed: 14·5 knots.
Complement: 111.   Built: 1915.

At least one ex 1915 minesweeper plus smaller launches were used for surveying duties.

METEOR   PAUL BENEKE

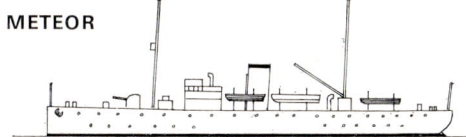

PAUL BENEKE   Navigation School Tender
460 tons; 165 (OA) × 25, 12½ knots. Crew: 30.   Built: 1936.

YACHTS

Grille   1938

GRILLE   State Yacht
Displacement: 2,560 tons.
Dimensions: 377 (OA) × 44.
Armament: 3 × 4·1 inch, 2 × 37mm, plus 20mm.
Speed: 20 knots, 8,000 SHP.
Complement: 245.   Built: 1934.

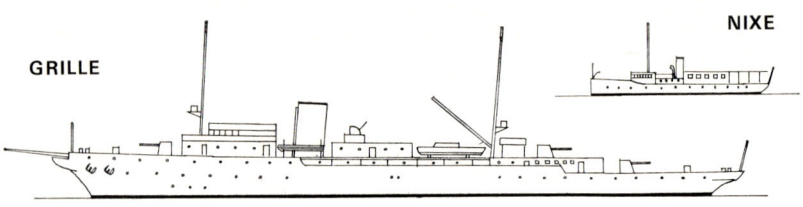

NIXE   Commander-in-Chief's Yacht
108 tons; 97 (OA) × 16½; 13 knots. Crew: 13.   Built: 1914.

MISCELLANEOUS

DRACHE   Gunnery Training Tender
790 tons; 176 (OA) × 32; 6 × 4·1 inch, 20mm; 18 knots. Crew: 69.
Note: Some ex 1915 minesweepers also used in this role.

MT1, MT2   Minelaying Tenders
550 tons; 164 (OA) × 30; 10 knots. Crew: 48.   Built: 1917.

ORKAN   Tug
470 tons; 120 (OA) × 34; 10 knots. Crew: 22.   Built: 1916.
Note: There were numerous small harbour and coastal tugs.

DRACHE 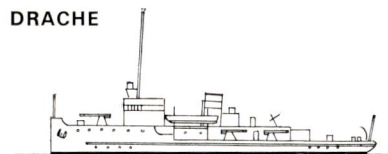   Ex-Torpedo Boat

Ex World War 1 Torpedo Boats
There were 14 of these ships and, although long past operational use in their original role, performed various duties including tenders to submarines, gunnery and torpedo training. Typical data: 800 tons, 240 (OA) × 25; 1 or 2 = 4·1 inch; up to 4 torpedo tubes; 22 to 31 knots. Crew: 80.

6107 (ex-Torpedo Boat)   1939

ACHERON, GAZELLE, FRAUNLOB, HECHT, JAGD, DELPHIN Tenders
Displacement: 525 tons.
Dimensions: 192 (OA) × 24.
Armament: 1 × 4·1 inch in some, plus small AA.
Speed: 16 knots.
Note: All ex-World War I minesweepers, built 1917–19, that were converted into tenders for various rôles as shown: **Acheron** (Submarines), **Delphin** (Gunnery) the remainder were used for general duties. Some (see drawing) had a poop deck added. See page 63 for picture and other ships which remained in the minesweeping rôle.

'Acheron' class 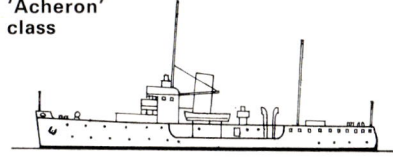   NORDSEE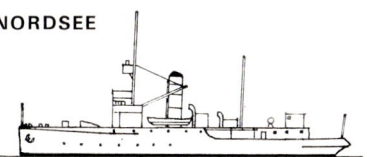

NORDSEE Navigational Training Tender
Displacement: 830 tons.
Dimensions: 176 × 31.
Armament: Light AA.
Speed: 12 knots.
Note: Built in 1914 as a minesweeper and converted to a tender, for navigation training, in 1935.

NETTLEBECK
General Training Tender

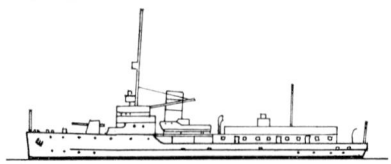

Displacement: 550 tons.
Dimensions: 184 × 24.
Armament: 1 × 4·1 inch, Light AA.
Speed: 12 knots.
Note: Built in 1919 as a minesweeper and converted to tender, for general training duties (see extra superstructure on drawing), before the war.

LUMME   Diving Tender
Displacement: 62 tons.
Dimensions: 85 × 15.
Speed: 9 knots.
Complement: 9.

'C' Class   Minelaying Tenders
120 tons, 9 knots. Small ships used for ferrying mines to other ships and servicing them.

Energie, Ausdauer   IWM-HU3303   1940

ENERGIE, AUSDAUER   Submarine Salvage Ships
These were two specially built vessels for submarine rescue and recovery work. They had heavy lift winches and derricks, salvage equipment, and decompression chambers.

OIL TANKERS

There were many ex-Merchant Service tankers requisitioned for coastal and harbour supply work, carrying fuel for the operational fleet. These included the following major units:

SAMLAND   (10,100 tons).

BROSEN   (2,500 tons).

WOLLIN   (3,500 tons).

MINE TRANSPORTS

A class of purpose-built ships was put in service specifically for carrying mines and other explosives for the operational fleet. These ships were:

LAUTING, RHEIN, OTTER, IRBEN
(All 1,253 tons).

The supply ship Altmark (page 74) lying in Alten Fjord, Norway, in February 1940 at about the time of the boarding by HMS Cossack in a successful bid to rescue imprisoned British seamen from the Graf Spee.

Appendix 1: Officers' Ranks

SLEEVE INSIGNIA

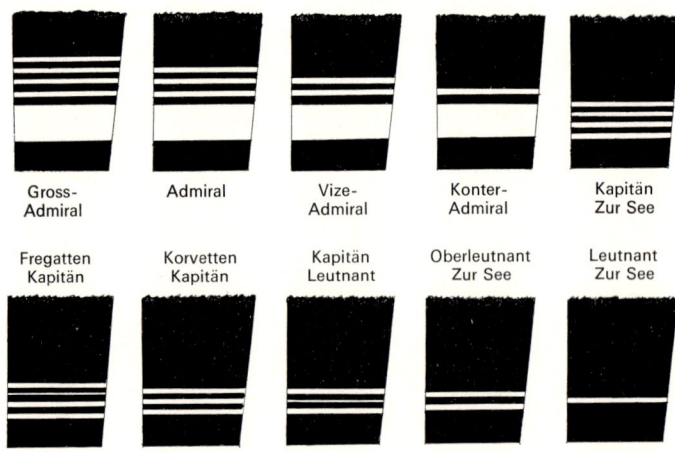

SPECIALIST BADGES

Executive   Engineer

Accountant   Medical

(Worn above rank bands)

EQUIVALENT RANKS

German	British
Grossadmiral	Admiral of the Fleet
Admiral	Admiral
Vizeadmiral	Vice-Admiral
Konteradmiral	Rear Admiral
Kapitän Zur See	Captain
Fregatten Kapitän	Commander
Korvetten Kapitän	Lieutenant-Commander
Kapitän-Leutnant	Lieutenant (senior)
Oberleutnant Zur See	Lieutenant (junior)
Leutnant Zur See	Sub-Lieutenant

Appendix 2: Naval Flags

Jack and National Flag

Naval Ensign

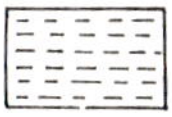

Red

The end of another patrol as the crew of a Type VIIC U-boat come on deck to enter harbour. The conning tower is decorated with a flotilla emblem, the cat, and a tally of claimed sinkings by the boat. Putting to sea in the other direction is a flotilla of minesweepers (IWM).

Notes